Daring to Share

8 Brave Souls
Sharing
Their Authentic
Road Trip

™

DIANA REYERS

Connecting Humanity Through the Art of Storytelling

Volume 1

DARING TO SHARE

CONNECTNG HUMANITY ONE STORY AT A TIME

DIANA REYERS

AUTHENTICITY COACH
STORYTELLER | CONNECTOR | HUMAN ADVOCATE

Published by Daringly Mindful, October, 2018
ISBN: 9781999401009

Editor: Diana Reyers
Typeset: Greg Salisbury
Book Cover Design: Judith Mazari

THE
DEDICATION

™

By Diana Reyers

My life would be incredibly incomplete without
my husband, Hank, by my side.
He will never fully comprehend how impactful his quiet and
constant way of encouraging my personal evolution has been.
He is the love of my life and much more than
I ever thought I was worthy of.

My children inspire me to show up in the world
from a place of truth.
Each of them taught me that being vulnerable and sharing
how we truly feel is the most impactful way to connect
genuinely with another human being.
Simon, Olivia and Nik, I am grateful for the
laughter and meaningful conversations
we share while breaking bread around our dinner table.
I want you to know that you are my world.

My Family Is My Greatest Blessing And
The Reason You Are Holding This Book In Your Hands

PRAISE FOR
THE BOOK

™

*"Most of us have secrets, memories, and past actions; feelings and
deeds hidden from friends, strangers, and sometimes even from
ourselves; that were they exposed we would be mortified!
Especially as an actress, director, and as a fellow author, I have
to be willing to stand stripped bare of the safety of a mask - and
instead share these same vulnerabilities portrayed within each
character for the world to see.
Amazed pleasantly as if I am observing snowflakes fall to the
ground and yet defy the expectation of melting, I absorb the
phenomenal courage by those who pour open the depths of their
souls in these beautiful stories before you which
you now have the opportunity to share.
I applaud them."*

DIANE LADD
Actress | Director | Writer
International Award Winner, including British Academy
Award and 3X Oscar Nominee.
Author — "Spiraling Through the School of Life",
Hay House Publisher and
"A Bad Afternoon for a Piece of Cake"
A Collection Ten short stories, Exxcell Publisher
www.dianeladd.com

PRAISE FOR
THE BOOK

"*Inspiring stories shared by these 8 brave men and women reflect an intuitive calling to surrender to the truth within. Truth is a funny little word that has depths so deep we can't see them at first glance so, we have to walk toward them, into them, to know them. It takes suffering, strength and courage to walk this road with eyes wide open...you will find yourself, here.*"

**Heather Haynes Artist and Philanthropist
Owner of Heather Haynes Gallery
Creator of the Walls of Courage
Founder of Worlds Collide Africa**

"*The stories in this book are vulnerable, real and daring. As a publisher I am always encouraging my authors to have the courage to really dig deep and be authentic in their journey, but rarely this happens because judgement gets in the way. Diana has a unique gift to encourage these authors to tell their stories from this place, and the results are sometimes shockingly dareful! Congratulations Diana, you have inspired a group of storytellers to share their journeys to encourage others to learn from their experiences.*"

Julie Salisbury Publisher, Influence Publishing

By Diana Reyers

Tana Heminsley is my beacon of hope.
Through all the chaos in this world, she continuously
shares and shows me there is a better way;
a way that empowers me and others to choose to lead an
authentic life with conscious intention.
I am honoured to call Tana my mentor and friend and her
ALG tribe, my community of support.

Jane Tohill is my soul mate and life-long bestie.
Through laughter, tears, outrageous adventures,
and complete acceptance of one another,
we achieved the honour to celebrate
infinite and deep friendship.
I feel deep gratitude having received our unique bond.

Scott De Freitas-Graff and John De Freitas
Daring to Share, The Movement would never have evolved
had it not been for the unconditional support
of my island besties.
Scott is my spirit animal; John is my blessing friend.
I hold a special place in my heart for each of these
loving and kind individuals.

IX

Julie Salisbury is a publisher extraordinaire and
an author's dream come true.
She is that beautiful soul everyone wishes to cross paths with.
I thank Julie for respecting my creative mind and individuality
while having faith in the intention of this project.

The Universe is my greatest inspiration.
The forest is my sanctuary, the place I take to
and find clarity in;
the trees, rocks, roots, moss, wind and the sky
that surround me as I move within, around and
through every nook and cranny of it.
I will never take for granted its incredible gift of
taking me to creative freedom
while providing the blessing to thrive from my soul, my truth.

THE
CONTENTS

THE
FOREWORD

TM

by Tana Heminsley

The Journey from "There to Here" or becoming your Authentic self, is the pathway to personal freedom. This is your birthright and potential and what may have gotten lost as a result of experiences and the influence of others to this point in your life.

Diana describes how to think of the journey from "There to Here" as "There" being a place of unconsciously showing up as one's inauthentic self, and "Here" being a place of consciously showing up within one's authenticity .

When you rediscover who you are as your authentic or best self, connected to universal energy in each moment of presence, life changes. As you remember and cultivate your true self or essence more of the time, you slow down, experience more ease, and become very intentional. Over time you make different choices – self-nurturing and incredible choices that allow who you are and what is important to you, to shine through in more moments of each day.

This personal journey requires years if not decades of awareness, personal growth and development. It is not for the faint of heart. It requires continuous courage to delve deep into the patterns of the personality or ego and to make choices about which to keep and which to let go of along the way. It often requires support from a variety of sources which may show up in the most synchronistic of ways. And it requires empowering conversations with self and others, setting boundaries and living in ways that are congruent with what is deeply important to you.

This is what you will experience as you open the pages to each chapter and each contributor's story.

When Diana told me several years ago she was going to write a book, it didn't surprise me.

It didn't surprise me because over the 7 years we have known each other, each time Diana said she was going to do something, she did it – whether it was planning and carrying out a move across the country with her family, or training to become an Authentic Leadership Conversation™ Facilitator and offering this to her clients in record time, developing her version of the Authentic You™ Personal Planning System which she called the "Authentic Road Trip" program and supporting many others to discover their authentic selves, or creating the sacred space for storytelling where people can share their journeys "with nothing but a stool, a microphone and a glass of water by their side" – she says she is going to do something, and then she does it.

Diana is an incredibly inspiring, heart-centred, purpose-focused activator and connector. She gets things done, and she creates community wherever she goes.

What did surprise me though was just how much I would be both moved while at the same time deeply inspired by each contributor when I savoured their stories. Several, I read more than once, and many moved me to tears – both of sadness as I felt their lows, and contentment as I felt their arrival at their final destination – here.

I was honoured when she asked me to write a chapter for her book and to tell my story of "From There to Here". And, then she asked me to write the Foreword; I was honoured once again.

Diana's purpose for this book is to introduce you to 8 people who are committed enough and willing to put themselves out there in spite of the incredible vulnerability of speaking their truth and sharing the story of their journeys with you.

It is also to have you experience what Diana has called the "Inner Purpose Feeling" – or the one emotion that you feel when you are aware and experiencing your authentic self, and that is aligned with your values and provides guideposts for an authentic approach to living.

So, grab your courage, along with a cup of tea, and be prepared to be moved and to feel like you want to have a deeper conversation with each of the people who have written a chapter of this book.

Diana's final intention for it is to create a movement for humanity and connection where we join together to "support one another through Conversation™ as we share and listen with love and respect, honouring our stories, one by one, Daring to Share."

She has accomplished it in her book and did it with authenticity and ease.

Tana Heminsley
Author "Awaken Your Authentic Leadership –
Lead with Inner Clarity and Purpose"
CEO and Founder, Authentic Leadership Global

Tana Heminsley is a master at the practical application — the how — of emotional intelligence and Authentic Leadership. Both support leaders to heal old wounds and improve their effectiveness while experiencing more ease — in the workplace and at home.

Her career has included roles such as :

- founding Authentic Leadership Global™ – an online-based business supporting organizations to transform their culture through individual and team growth and development.
- facilitating leadership development for 1000's of leaders through ViRTUS.
- being a member of the Executive team for BC Hydro – one of North America's leading providers of clean, renewable energy – with 4,500 employees, annual net income of $400 Million (2007) and 1.7 million customers.
- consulting for the founders of the balanced scorecard management system, which originated out of Harvard, and
- starting, owning and selling "Tana Lee" a retail clothing store.

Tana holds an Executive MBA from Simon Fraser University, Vancouver, B.C. Canada, a PCC credential with International Coach Federation, is an Integral Coach trained through New Ventures West, a Certified Professional EQ Analyst, a Certified Authentic Leadership Program Facilitator and has trained on the Enneagram.

THE INTRODUCTION

by Diana Reyers

I began writing this book more than 20 years ago. I was, initially, writing about me and my life-long journey of seeking the courage to show up in the world as my unique self. So many years ago, I knew my story would be about my road trip of *From There to Here* but, I didn't have clarity about what I did within that road trip or how to articulate it. Over the years, I started and stopped writing many times. I was unclear about where the story would take me or how it would end. I focused solely on what happened in my story while neglecting how those chronological events affected me emotionally and spiritually. It took me 2 decades, much reflection and many U-turns to discover that my story is not about what I do within it, but instead, how I feel as I move through it, and then, how I respond to my intuition.

Through my experience as a *Certified Authentic Leadership Program Facilitator*™ I discovered that people do not find fulfillment or joy within their *doing*, but rather in how they are *feeling*. We do not find a true understanding of ourselves based on the list of things we have to accomplish on any given day. Once we reach the point of being able to grab our courage to look beyond the things we have to do, we see ourselves as a physical capsule holding a cornucopia of emotions and beliefs that are uniquely ours and that deserve to be honoured. We begin to choose to connect to our soul, the part of us that is difficult to describe but, that defines us as our most genuine version. We seek the clarity and confidence to show up within an Authentic way of being, one that reflects our personal values and honours the same in others.

Initially, we may not recognize that our emotions mirror our values which simultaneously, create guideposts towards decisiveness about how we want to show up in the world. However, once we achieve that awareness, we find the clarity about who we are and how we feel within our unique evolution. This discovery can change everything about the choices we make as human beings because we are exactly that, beings who are human. We have hearts and souls that carry emotions, passions, needs and wants with a deep knowing about how we want to feel and be as an individual amongst many. I call this being aware of our *Inner Purpose Feeling*. It is the unique feeling each of us yearns to experience most of the time. If there is a Fairy God Mother, and she was able to tap you on the head with her wand and bestow one emotion upon you to experience for the rest of your life, what feeling would you choose? This is your *Inner Purpose Feeling*, and it takes time, acute awareness and complete vulnerability to discover what it is for you and what transpires from committing to its truth.

Relying on a feeling may seem unreliable in a world that often depends on the validity of science alone. However, paying attention to how we feel, physically and emotionally, provides us with the ability to slow down and reflect on the *why* of what we are experiencing, good or bad. Our bodies and our emotions are the first and second receivers of any indication that we are being or not being true to ourselves; this is the time to pay attention as we either receive messages of confident decisiveness and contentment or the chatter of anxious indecisiveness and chaos. Slowing down to listen provides the space of time and energy to recalibrate and shift to how we really want to show up. However, ignoring our feelings can move us to self-deception and to a way of showing up that creates possible trade-offs of mental and physical ill-health and disease as our discomfort manifests within us. At some point, we reach our capacity and we can break.

The *Inner Purpose Feeling* provided me and my clients with something to think about and utilize within moments, days, months and years of indecisiveness. Once they determined their *Inner Purpose Feeling* and became aware of when they were NOT experiencing it, they suddenly became hyperaware that something was amiss; what value was being compromised in that moment? They were able to determine what or who was blocking their ability to feel what they wanted to feel, their Inner Purpose Feeling, and then move towards that emotion by responding effectively to the person or situation within their truth. The feeling came before the doing, and they were able to, consciously, determine what that feeling meant to them. With this awareness in place, they had the confidence to choose to shift and show up within their authenticity, from a heartfelt place within their self, with decisiveness, confidence and ease, and connected to their soul. The awareness provided them with the ability to practice Social and Emotional Intelligence; living their truth while honouring that of others. Empowerment combined with Compassion.

Once I articulated, practiced and saw the positive results of coaching this pragmatic mindfulness technique to hundreds of individuals, I realized this book could never be just about me. It needed to be a collaborative project sharing many human stories of *From There to Here*; *There* being a place of unconsciously showing up as one's inauthentic self, and *Here* being a place of consciously showing up within one's authenticity. The journey in between describes incredibly challenging obstacles and the painful emotional turmoil each writer experiences while striving for their cathartic and freeing destination.

This book's intention is to share how I and each of the storytellers *Dared to Share* the discovery of our courage in order to move through our *From There to Here* using our *Inner Purpose Feeling* towards finding our Authentic Selves within adversities that many cannot fathom managing. Within the inspiration, some of the storylines may trigger discomfort for the reader as all the stories are told from a place of complete truth and vulnerability while practicing compassion for all those involved.

I had conversations, too many to count, with a multitude of individuals eager to throw their personal lives out into the world. When asked why they wanted to commit to and experience such vulnerability, every one of them believed that if their story could move someone towards the feeling of leading a more authentic life, it was worth the personal exposure.

This is unlike any other collaborative book you will read as you *feel* the writer more than you care about what she or he is *doing* surrounding that experience. As a collective, the authors decided never to tell you what you should do or how you should be or feel. We believe that is for you to decide. However, if the writers inspire you to find your own way, your own *Inner Purpose Feeling*, then we have accomplished what we set out to do.

Our mandate is not to provide you with the motivation

to succeed in business, find long-lasting love or determine your life's purpose because that will happen naturally as you become motivated to commit to your own *Authentic Road Trip*. We created this collection of stories to provide you with the inspiration to discover how you choose to feel connected to your self, others and the entire universe – this will become your unique road trip, your *From There To Here*.

Each storyteller discovered which emotion articulated his or her *Inner Purpose Feeling* while writing their story. You may experience this feeling as you move through the vulnerability of their sharing. Each chapter represents our individual Authentic Road Trip and the feeling we land within at the end of our journey. Collectively, we discovered the feelings of Love, Faith, Integrity, Belonging, Calm, Grace, Inner Peace and Truth, a string of emotions that rested in our souls for a very long time, waiting to be trusted and released.

For me, authenticity translates into my *Inner Purpose Feeling* of Truth. When I choose to listen to and trust my soul, I muster up the courage to allow it to guide me towards what is real and right for me. I don't need a reason to have faith in it other than because it feels right within my physical, emotional and spiritual self; it is my truth, what's not to trust? The first time I surrendered to this mindset, I was scared to death. But, the more I practiced listening to my truth, I began honouring the truth of others as well; it very quickly became second nature to me. My life became balanced in every way as I experienced the ease that comes with letting go of self-deceit.

In collaboration with my beautiful and loving friend, Scott De Freitas-Graff, *Daring to Share, Volume 1*, the Book expanded into the Event[1]. Along with our upcoming book

---

[1] Find *Daring to Share* storytelling and book launch events and information at daringtoshare.com

launches featuring our authors, it is offered several times a year bringing 6 members of our community together to share their stories in person within courage and vulnerability. A strong yearning developed as people from all walks of life gathered to experience connection created by something so very real and raw.

We successfully fulfilled our intention of *Connecting Humanity Through the Art of Storytelling* by sharing an ordinary person's *From There to Here* with nothing but a stool, a microphone and a glass of water by their side.

But, *Daring to Share* is so much more than storytelling. It is a Movement supporting humanity in keeping things simple as we walk through this life experience together, one step at a time and with ease. We, being us, you and I, all the human beings in the world doing the best we can every day to support one another through Conversation and Connection as we share and listen with love and respect, honouring our stories, one by one; we are *Daring to Share*.

Photo by ML Kenneth

FROM THERE TO HERE

INTRODUCING
JOY KINGSBOROUGH

I met Joy Kingsborough in the fall of 2014 at a business meeting where I was giving a presentation on authenticity. While speaking, I remember glancing up at Joy, and she was smiling and nodding her head in, what I interpreted, agreement with what I was saying.

It was after the talk, and when I met Joy in person, that I realized her gestures extended far beyond a mutual agreement of the topic to more of a compassionate, supportive intention to welcome me and make me feel comfortable within her and group's presence.

It is not a mystery that Joy chose Love as her Inner Purpose Feeling to guide her through her life's journey. Joy is the definition of Love as she shows up in this world being, doing, and moving from a place of Love no matter what or who comes her way. Personally, I am blessed to have met Joy, and I am honoured to call her my friend. Once you experience her Authentic Road Trip, she will suddenly become your friend as well; she just manages to do that!!

You are about to experience Joy's Story of
From There to Here **and how she discovered the feeling of**
Love

Diane Roger

1

From There to Here;

LOVE

By Joy Kingsborough

Love

TM

Joy's Story

The year 2002 marks the most difficult and the most transformational year of my life. It stands out as the most difficult time, not because circumstances were worse than earlier years but, because this was the time in my life when I finally said, "enough is enough." My neatly tucked away emotions were beginning to surface in uncomfortable and destructive ways. I was being reckless with my finances, neglecting my health, and putting myself in dangerous situations with men I didn't know. I was miserable and recognized that I couldn't live like this anymore.

Like many people, my past is filled with traumatic events, events that I was unprepared to deal with using the mind of a small child. Because of this limited capacity, instead of processing my pain, I became an expert at defaulting to hiding it. I believed that my life was meant to be hard and that I should accept my reality and be grateful just to be alive. At the time, I believed this ill-fated destiny, except that every now and then, I had this little voice inside my head that would quietly whisper to me, "You are meant for more than this". The voice was subliminal for many years and I chose to ignore her; I thought I could push her down forever. But, I was wrong because, over time, that voice became louder and much more persistent, and I was unable to compartmentalize it any longer. I am glad that my little voice didn't give up as it, eventually, became my most trusted ally and guide. Over time, I became desperate for my life to end so that I wouldn't have to endure the pain any longer. I saw no way out, but to leave this world. If someone were to tell me then that I would now be supporting others to master their own emotions and live truly joyful and fulfilling lives, I would never have believed them. I would never have believed that I would, not only be okay but, also truly happy. What I am sharing now is the story of my journey out of the depths of hell into the loving embrace of my own self-love.

We've all been 'There', or at least some version of what 'There' is. My version was a period of time, not so long ago, when my whole world came crashing down around me. I hit rock bottom and I discovered that I needed to choose to, either surrender and heal, or disappear into the oblivion of depression. This all happened during that most difficult life changing year of 2002. I dreaded waking up in the morning and I drank myself to sleep in the evening. I couldn't stand the sound of my own thoughts. When I got up in the morning and looked in the mirror, I cried. This all came from my default pattern of locking my past up in the recesses of my mind, memories that

I safely hid from my consciousness for nearly 30 years.

Until one day, when those memories came flooding back in a truly unexpected moment on a desert road in Arizona. I was driving to my mother's house for a visit; we lived 2 hours apart and I made the drive to see her as often as possible. It began to rain as I drove down the highway, and amidst the background sound of the raindrops on my windshield, something began to stir inside me. It was the same feeling I've had when leaving the water running in the bathroom while quickly finishing something else in another room. Unconsciously, you remember that the water is running but, you think you have plenty of time before it overflows. Then, from one moment to the next, you completely forget about the running water, and it, unexpectedly, begins to flood. As I was driving down the road that day, that sudden feeling of urgency is what I felt. But, this time it wasn't the water overflowing from my tub, it was, instead, my tears filling up inside of me getting ready to spill over. I had no emotional capacity to restrain them any longer.

I didn't understand what was happening and I was scared. I had learned to control my emotions, and the inevitability of what was about to happen felt foreign and frightening to me. At this time in my life, I believed that crying was weak, even for women. Growing up, my father told me many times, "If you want to succeed in business you cannot be emotional." He followed that ridiculous statement with a more direct and personal message that I was "Too emotional."

"The message I received and believed was, "Joy you will never succeed in business if you show your emotions to the world."

So, I wore that badge with deep dedication, and kept

myself stoic and emotionally small. Business was always my passion, even before I became an entrepreneur. I love to mold ideas into something useful for the world. It ignites my deeper purpose and passion for life. Yet, I was struggling to fit in to Corporate America. I was working in high level roles, side by side with some of the smartest minds in Telecommunications, mostly men who dominated that corporate arena. I desperately wanted their respect so, I focused on my masculine traits of ambition and drive while I suppressed my feminine traits of intuition and emotional vulnerability. I now know that I was squashing who I really am in order to gain acceptance, the same acceptance I craved from my father. I wanted to prove to my father that I wasn't too emotional and I could be successful in business if I showed up as a strong woman and just worked harder like men did. I later discovered that suppressing any aspect of who I am is a recipe for failure.

The raindrops hitting my windshield that day triggered those repressed emotions which gave way to an overwhelming release of tears. I couldn't see through my tears or my windshield. The raindrops seemed to fall in unison with my tears, and I couldn't wipe them away any faster than my windshield wipers could clear the rain. I felt like I was in the midst of a flash flood and needed to pull over to safety. I knew that I could not block what was happening and that I needed to provide myself with the space to truly feel this experience. With the flood of tears, came the memories. I saw the first man who abused me when I was 6 years old. I was at my first sleep over with a friend from kindergarten. I was so excited about this new experience, and could hear my dad's words in my head, "Make sure you are on your best behavior so, they will want to invite you back". I was a good little girl. Even though I didn't like it, I ate everything at dinner. I said "Please" and "Thank you." I cleaned up after myself, and everyone seemed to be happy to have me. The beginnings of my people-pleasing were well in place. So, that evening when I was fast asleep and my friend's father came into my room, I didn't dare say no; I wanted to behave.

The whole memory flooded back as I sat in my car on the side of the road weeping in unison with the rain. I felt every physical and emotional feeling I had when he touched me so long ago. Every thought in my 6-year-old mind flooded my 30-year old mind as if I was reliving the experience in that moment. I even remembered how I felt after he left the room. I remember hiding in the closet, afraid that he would come back. In the morning, my friend found me laying against a pile of toys and clothes laughing at me for falling asleep in the closet; more shame. I remember her telling her family at breakfast how funny it was that I had slept walked and ended up in the closet. I never said a word that morning sitting at their kitchen table, and I never told anyone what really happened. I tucked it all away in a dark corner of my mind to protect and preserve; I had to be a strong, good little girl. I sat on the side of the road in reflection, and after a time, the memory faded. I began to see new reasons for my life experiences and why I said and chose what I did. I saw and understood myself for the first time. I woke up from the unconscious life I was living and saw everything from a higher perspective. I realized what I had been running from my whole life. There was a degree of freedom in finally understanding why I didn't like men while, simultaneously, longing for their love and approval.

But, my journey did not begin or end with that moment on the side of the road. After months of personal work, the epiphany I had was a pivotal moment in my healing, however, I still had many miles to travel before I would experience complete freedom. This was just the beginning as my father's words were still branded in my mind. There were so many things in my life that needed to be undone before I could move forward. I knew I needed to let go of my father and his influence in my life, and especially, my thoughts. There were also other hidden details from my past that needed to be unveiled and faced. He was wrong about telling me to block my emotions and he was wrong about me but, I didn't believe that until years later. My journey to that awareness took me down a winding, twisting road of self-discovery, pain and, finally and ultimately, love.

What I didn't realize at the time was that everything I experienced since I was born brought me to this moment. I didn't have just one traumatic experience that triggered my life to spiral. The spiraling began my first day on this earth, the day I was born. My entry into the world exposed me to stress, anxiety and pain. My mother had a difficult pregnancy that included hypertension; she was beyond uncomfortable as her entire body was swollen while waiting 3 weeks past her due date for her baby to arrive. When she finally went into labor, it did not go smoothly, and her life was in danger. She was rushed from her local hospital in a rural Wisconsin town to a larger hospital in Minnesota where she and I would have a better chance of surviving. It was anything but a dream delivery, and I imagine it was traumatic and frightening for both of my parents. I always felt that I came into the world with a strong connection to stress and anxiety. I remember being worried about everything at a very young age, and I felt a sense of worry and dread hanging over every situation I encountered. I searched for meaning in life before I was old enough to understand what I was looking for. I remember making up stories and telling lies as a way of making myself feel better and to help make sense of life. If I didn't like something, I just pretended it didn't happen and told people grand stories that I convinced myself were true.

This created a cycle of experiencing one difficult situation after another, ignoring my feelings, ignoring what was happening, and making up new stories along the way.

It's now easy to see why I preferred and created my make-believe world instead of facing and accepting real life events. I was exposed to sexuality before the age of 5, molested at 6, and raped by a schoolmate at a party as a 15-year-old teenager. During my teen years, I was threatened both sexually and emotionally many times and physically assaulted by my first serious boyfriend. I never told anyone, and as I grew into adulthood, I forgot most of what happened and moved on.

"I believe I compartmentalized the significant memories related to these abusive experiences, and eventually, the remaining memories became fractured."

There were times when I remembered pieces of what happened and felt haunted by the pieces I didn't. I remembered my father telling me to be strong and not to show emotions; the stories I made up became my support and defense against the fear of being weak if I shared the emotional pain I had endured. My fantasy world helped me barricade my truth and manage moving through the motions of everyday life. However, I did not properly deal with my past, and the result was chronic, daily anxiety and fear. It seemed that the more I put off facing the truth, the more difficult situations manifested in my life and I spiraled further and further into darkness.

I met my fiancé in my late 20's after one failed marriage and raising a 5-year old on my own. I believed my prayers for love and support had been answered. This man loved me and my son unconditionally, owned a business of his own, had a strong financial foundation and the desire to give back to others. He wanted to take care of me and erase all the pain of my past. It was a time of hopefulness and possibility, and it seemed like my dreams were being fulfilled. Unfortunately, he had an advanced form of cancer and I was in denial; back to that pattern of make-believe. I shopped for a wedding dress and a place to be married while he went to doctors' appointments and recovered from chemotherapy treatments. I managed to convince myself this was all normal and he would recover. I did what I always did as I made up half-truths to help me cope with the ugly aspects of what was happening. I really believed that my intense love for my fiancé and my daily prayers to God would outweigh the inevitable truth that he was dying. I believed that I was the victim of a terrible situation and because I was such a good person, I would be rescued and he would be saved. My fiancé died, and my life lost all meaning. My dream of a happy life disappeared just like that!! I wanted to die too. I didn't want to stay in this cruel world with a God who betrayed me like this. I didn't believe there was anything left for me. My whole life was a painful blur, and I believed my family and friends were better off without me. I truly believed the thoughts I had, and I didn't believe I could survive any longer. I merely went through the motions; I felt dead inside. Every day, I got out of bed, took my son to school, went to work, came home, made dinner, and then went to sleep. I slept a lot.

My first attempt to kill myself happened spontaneously. I was driving home from work with my 6-year old son in the backseat of the car. I found myself crossing a bridge, and in an instant of what felt like bravery, I began moving towards the side of the bridge. For a moment, I blanked out as I obsessed over the many things that had gone wrong in my life and all the pain I had experienced; I wanted that pain to end, and I forgot my son was with me. As I neared the edge of the bridge, something transformative happened to me. I heard a voice and felt a nudge from within me. In an instant, I looked up and caught a glimpse of my son in the rear-view mirror; my beautiful, innocent boy. My love for him was enough to shake me from my insanity quickly enough to correct my path and get back on the road. Thankfully, I listened to that voice from within me because had I not seen my son in the mirror that day, I don't know what would have happened. I don't like thinking about it but, in that instant, I knew I wasn't okay. I knew I was suffering from depression and I was suicidal but, I didn't know how to ask for help. I didn't believe anyone could truly understand what I was feeling, and I thought I may not be able to be helped. So, I remained silent like I always had. My helplessness and self-hatred were fueled even more, and my desire to end my own life escalated.

One night, my son was with his father, and I was home alone. I ran a bath, lit candles, put on soft music, poured a tall glass of vodka and lemonade and used it to take a handful of pain pills. They were a saved bottle from a surgery I had years ago. I measured the dose carefully and knew exactly the amount I would need to ensure a successful death. I slipped into the bath and began to cry. The tears didn't last long, and when they subsided, I began to feel euphoric; the painkillers were kicking in, and I felt sort of hazy and numb. I surrendered to the feelings of peace, and eventually, the heaviness of sleep. I remember having one last thought before passing out, I didn't want people to find me in the bathtub naked. Somehow, that motivated me to get out of the water, into my pajamas and into my bed. That's the last thing that I remember until the next morning. I woke up in my own bed feeling sick, disoriented, confused and very much alive. It didn't work! I am filled with gratitude for the unseen force that kept me alive but, that morning I was the opposite of grateful. I felt betrayed and hopeless. I felt powerless and more alone than ever. Looking back, I realize that this unsuccessful attempt at taking my life made suicide an impossibility, and it was the last time I tried.

With suicide a pointless option, I learned to cope with my worsening depression using food, and I began to feel better. Food became my best friend and my greatest ally to ease my grief and pain. When I ate comforting food, I felt whole again. Food filled the emptiness in me for a while but, I needed more within a few hours. I transferred feeling bad about my life and my past to feeling bad about my body. In many ways, I chose food to save my life only to discover that it betrayed me by providing me with a new problem, obesity.

In the 2 years that followed I gained 100 pounds. I felt worthless and alone. Yet, despite my self-loathing, I saw a glimmer of hope within me and dreamt of being genuinely happy one day. I felt that if I lost my excess weight, I would finally find happiness again. My desire to lose weight became my obsession. One afternoon, while lying on the couch binge eating and watching The Oprah Winfrey Show, I was introduced to the book that would impact me more than any other book I have ever read. Oprah had become my life-line to hope, and she provided me with an escape from my life; I never missed her show. During this particular episode, Oprah introduced a new guest, Dr. Phillip McGraw[2]. He was promoting his new book, *Self Matters*[3]. I was mesmerized by his blunt yet, loving words. Dr. Phil seemed to be speaking to me directly through the television that day. He told me that I was the only one who could change my life. He also said that I was responsible for how others treated me and what came into my life. He

---

[2]You can find more about Dr. Phillip McGraw at drphil.com
[3]You can find Self Matters by Phillip C. McGraw PHD at drphilstore.com

let me know that It was up to me to decide what I was going to do with my life, who was in it, and how I responded to it all. He told me that I wasn't the victim of anything unless I allowed myself to be. His message of hope and change was revolutionary for me at the time. I instantly wondered how my life might look like if I wasn't the victim of my circumstances. It sparked something deep within me. I became aware of a source of motivation and self-love that I didn't know existed. I never wanted to fight for anything as much as I wanted to fight for myself that day.

Dr. Phil continued to speak sharing that his new book had helped so many people turn their lives around. I had a knowing that day that somehow this book would change my life. For the first time, I was ready to do whatever it took to make that happen. I got up from the couch and went to the bookstore and bought his book. I read it twice from cover to cover. Then, I bought a beautiful journal, went back to the book and completed the exercises one by one. I absorbed every question and answered them honestly; I began to notice patterns in my thinking and my life. Working through the exercises transformed my mindset and my self-worth. I saw a side of myself I had never acknowledged, and I noticed a bit of compassion rise up from within me. I suddenly believed in myself enough to attempt change, to investigate who I am from a vulnerable place, and to discover who the real Joy is.

As I worked through the book, I realized there may be psychological and emotional reasons for why I turned to food. At first, I believed that my rapid weight gain was the result of my recent past. At that point, I didn't realize the impact my past abuse had on my current journey to well-being. Instead, I associated all the pain I was carrying with the grief of losing my fiancé and attempting suicide. During the 2 years since he had passed, I gained more than 100 pounds and had sunk into depression. Before he died, I was a healthy weight and living my dream life. I had a family, a home, and someone to love me. It was easy to make the obvious connection that I gained weight due to the loss of the love of my life, rather than, see the underlying truth that the childhood abuse I endured created a need for self-protection through food. Although I didn't make this deeper connection at the time and I didn't reconcile the fractured memories yet, the beginning of my personal development journey was well underway, and there was no turning back from, what would end up being, a life time of self-discovery.

This self-discovery developed into a little more self-love with each passing day. I noticed that the more clarity I gained about what I, as an individual needed and wanted, the better I felt about myself. I observed that my thoughts and emotions were changing, and with those shifts, I felt inspired and compelled to eat differently and exercise. I found myself wanting to be kind to myself, and one day I woke up with a strong determination to lose weight in order to be healthy and honor who I was. I walked to work instead of driving, and I changed my eating habits to more healthy choices like drinking water instead of root beer. But, I think at this point of my journey from *There to Here*, the most integral shift was that I started a love affair with learning. I delved into absorbing everything I could about the way I thought and my mindset. I studied everything I could about my own physiology, biology and mind. I acquired certification as a personal trainer and nutrition consultant. I yearned to know everything about successful weight loss so, I could effectively maximize my efforts while maintaining wellness in all areas; emotionally, physically and spiritually. I wanted to create and be aware of the connections between my mind and body so I could sustain life-long weight loss. As a result of this clarity, I began to lose weight and it felt good. My self-esteem improved, and I was stronger than ever before.

"This is when I found myself sitting on the side of the road crying buckets of tears while experiencing the epiphany of why I was overweight; I had been hiding my emotions and my true self my whole life."

I realized that if I wanted to live a life guided by love, both for myself and others, I could not keep my soul in hiding any longer. This realization supported me to lose weight faster than any other time I had tried before, and I reached my weight goal in just a few months. It was almost effortless because I now knew why I never felt worthy of providing my body with good food and nutrition or my inner self with nurturance and compassion; all the abusers in my life taught me to be unworthy of anything that would make me feel loved. And so, that became the most significant part of my journey, learning to love myself bit by bit every day. It began with a morning ritual:

- Every morning after my shower, I applied lotion all over myself. As I massaged the lotion in, I spoke loving words to each body part; "Thank you, legs for carrying me through life, even with all of this extra weight."; "I love you, arms for always being there for me when I need you."
- I looked in the mirror and scanned my body from head to toe, even though I had to force myself in the

beginning; in the past, I only looked at specific areas that I did not like while feeling bad about myself. This new practice was very difficult for me as I did not want to acknowledge all of my body in its entirety. As I looked at my whole body, I found parts of me that I loved the most. Out loud, I said to the image, "I love my eyes", "I love my hair", "I love my arms".

- The last part of my ritual was the most difficult, and yet, the most transformational. Still standing before the mirror, I looked directly into my eyes and said, with as much honesty as possible, "I love you Joy."

I still do this all these years later.

Successfully loving myself and losing the weight is a direct result of my clarity about why I chose to sabotage my truth for so long. Knowing why enabled me to move beyond that mindset and shift the way I thought about myself and my self-worth. As a result, I created the willingness to do these small and loving things every day. No matter how hard it was or how silly I felt, I never allowed my doubts to control my truth. I loved myself a little more each day and the payback is immeasurable worthiness.

A year after discovering Dr. Phil's book, I transformed my thinking and lost 100 pounds. I left the career I hated and went back to school. I was a newlywed and felt more amazing than ever before in my life. All these changes happened in one year. In all my life, I was never so inspired, and I was in awe that my journey created this inspiration; I felt empowered! Like so many others who experience profound turn arounds in their lives, I wanted to share what I learned. I was so grateful to be alive and happy and to realize that I could choose this happiness without anyone or anything influencing how I felt.

I wanted others to know that they could feel the immense joy I was feeling. Birthed from my desire to share my experience, I felt the nudge to email Dr. Phil to tell him my story. In my email, I let him know how he impacted my life with his words of encouragement, how he helped me find self-esteem and create a healthy body. I poured my heart out, wanting him to know how important he was to me. I pushed my fear aside, and before I could stop myself, I hit the send button, and the email was on its way.

I pushed the email to the back of my mind until the next morning when I logged into my email account. Just like every other morning, I scanned my email subject lines for important messages. Suddenly, I saw an email from the Dr. Phil show. I looked twice at the sender's name before it registered that the email was from a producer at the Dr. Phil show. She asked if I would speak with her on the phone about my transformation; Dr. Phil read my email and wanted me to be a guest on an upcoming show! At first, I was in shock that I received a reply at all. Next, I got nervous about what they wanted to talk to me about. Finally, before I could stop myself, I wrote an email and hit the send button. I received a phone call 10 minutes later, and that conversation set a chain of whirlwind events into motion. Within days, camera crews from the Dr. Phil show came into my home, as well as, local news channels and representatives from my gym. People asked about my journey, my strategies, and my personal life. I was overwhelmed, yet excited, and I felt like I was living in a dream. My life was suspended during that time. I didn't work, but instead, posed for pictures, recorded video clips, appeared in advertisements and, eventually, flew to Los Angeles as a guest on the Dr. Phil show. They featured me as a "Success Story".

Driving through the gates at Paramount Studios, I felt like

I was in a dream. I met Dr. Phil's wife and other guests on the show backstage. My mom and best friend were flown in with me, and they watched from the audience as I walked on stage, met Dr. Phil and was interviewed for millions to watch. I was very nervous, and the entire experience is now mostly a blur. To this day, I have no idea what I said and have never watched the recording from the show. It was surreal and a milestone moment that I knew represented my entrance into a whole new life. The experience of being on the show was enough for me, and I honestly didn't know how my life would change after that time. I saw it as a moment of celebration and victory for the hard work I put into changing my life. I believed I would revel in the excitement and then life would go back to normal. Then, on January 19, 2003 the episode aired and the response to my appearance was completely unexpected. I received hundreds of emails and letters from people who watched the show, people who resonated with what I said. They asked me for guidance and support. I began to realize the impact my journey could have on the lives of others. I wasn't sure how to respond to all of them, and the producers of the show were encouraged to host a forum on the Dr. Phil website as a way for me to connect with people. Thank you again Dr. Phil! Posting online, I shared my advice and ideas and encouraged others to obtain their goals. This provided me with a sense of fulfillment that I didn't even know I wanted. I woke up excited every morning as I thought about what I would post and how I could help; I discovered my purpose.

I cannot imagine where my life would be today if I did not choose to start this journey so many years ago. I am just as grateful for the painful times as I am for the joyful because both led me to where I am today, Here. Even though my past played such a powerful and impactful role, I know I can let it go and make room for new life stories that are yet to unfold.

People often ask me, "Joy, what was your greatest lesson during that time?" My response is clearer today than ever before, my greatest lesson is that I am truly the love of my life and no thing, experience or person can cause me pain or make me happy. I am the master of my own fate, and I trust that love and happiness are an inside job. Dr. Phil didn't save me by writing that book or inviting me to appear on his show. Instead, he created an opportunity for me to save myself, and I chose to take it.

My purpose in this life is to be a living example of self-love. What started off as a journey to lose weight became something so much greater. It became a journey to save my life, a journey of self-discovery and self-love. I left There looking for something to ease my pain by ignoring my truth, only to arrive Here back to myself with the knowledge that I am the only source of love and happiness I will ever need. I could never have fully understood where I would end up when I was beginning my journey or that it could be this much fun! Now that I am here, I am delighted to know that the journey never really ends.

I DISCOVERED THE FEELING OF LOVE

HOW JOY INSPIRES LOVE

In 2003, Joy was inspired to leave corporate America in favor of a career that helped others. She established a conscious coaching practice working with hundreds of international clients. Joy used the wisdom from her past in combination with her education and professional background to intuitively guide people back to themselves.

Every day, Joy feels blessed with the opportunity to pay forward all that she experienced and learned. As she reflects on her life this far, she is in awe of how one decision can inspire someone to tap into their love of self and others and transform the course of an entire lifetime.

You can discover more about Joy, her signature programs,
a collaborative live life-changing annual event
and her new book,
Tarot-Numerology Archetypes
at joykingsborough.com

THE FOLLOWING STORIES BY
SCOTT DE FREITAS-GRAFF AND
JOHN DE FREITAS REFLECT
THEIR LOVE STORY AND THE
REDISCOVERY OF THEMSELVES
AMIDST A TUMULTUOUS TIME

INTRODUCING
SCOTT DE FREITAS GRAFF

Scott says that I am his Spirit Animal; I believe what he is saying is that we are connected from the soul. He is the Enthusiast or #7 in the Enneagram Personality Assessment, as am I. Together, we are 2 incredibly creative human beings bursting at the seams with thoughts, ideas and emotions, a chaotic explosion waiting to happen - a fireball of imagination that needs to be released, or who knows what will happen!! What has transpired is a beautiful Movement that is not ending any time soon!!

I like to think that I am a person who forgives easily and loves unconditionally but, Scott exceeds what I am capable of within this realm of compassion. He truly sees the best in everyone, sometimes to his detriment. But, if I could choose one of my flaws, I would pick the one he has chosen, to accept others unconditionally; he is a true beacon of Loving Kindness.

Scott is Daring to Share Movement's number one supporter as he consistently shows up for our weekly meetings preparing for our events and tours in addition to his day job. His love and loyalty are more than evident, and I am grateful for and value his friendship more than he may ever know.

You are about to experience Scott's Story of
From There to Here **and how he discovered the feeling of**
Integrity

Diane Boyer

From There to Here;

INTEGRITY

By Scott De Freitas-Graff

Integrity

™

Scott's Story

2017 was a turning point for me. It was the year I chose to say "YES!!" to everything. I embraced everything life threw at me with a "Joie de Vivre" that I never experienced before.

It started with Diana Reyers asking me to be a storyteller at the very first Dare to Share event in Oceanside on Vancouver Island, British Columbia where I live. I was terrified. Scared. To. Death. Who wants to hear my story? Who is even interested in my life? What do I have to offer? What if I stutter? What if I freeze? Oh my God!!

It took me 2 weeks to write my story. I was the last storyteller of the evening. I didn't enjoy listening to the other storytellers because, until the last moment, I was reviewing and rereading my notes. Then, the moment came when Diana introduced me to crowd of over 60 people. I took the mic from her hand and began to share my story. It was fantastic! I loved it! I let go completely and wouldn't shut up. It was at this point that I was bitten. I decided that, not only was I going to say "YES!!" to everything, I was going to throw caution to the wind and do things that scared the crap out of me. Being real, raw and vulnerable within our little community certainly fit that bill.

This also became a year of many triumphs and tremendous loss that forced me to re-evaluate my life. That very first Dare to Share event was the day before my 47th birthday. I lost a dear friend to a freak car accident a week later. He was 26 years old and left behind his parents and brother with whom I also had close relationships. I was overwhelmed with the pain, the loss and the feeling of helplessness. Often times, it's easier for me to be a human 'doing' as opposed to a human 'being'. So, with close mutual friends, I decided that we could, at the very least, alleviate some of the financial burden a sudden death like this brings. We set up a GoFundMe campaign, organized bottle drives, pub crawls and, with Diana's support, we turned the next Dare to Share into a fundraiser for my friend's family.

From there, I joined the board of a local community organization as public relations director. I threw myself into the many charity and community events this group provides. This fed my soul and, having felt disconnected for a very long time, provided me with, what would become, my theme for the year, connection.

A month after that, my father called me. His brother and best friend was in a coma and hospitalized that morning. My father was having a hard time managing the family, the hospital visits, and my mother who was suffering from stage 5 dementia. I could feel his pain, his own worry and sense of impending loss in his voice. My father, ever a strong man, was cracking under the pressure. I was on a plane bound for London eight hours later. We lost my uncle a few days after I arrived. He passed away quietly in the hospital surrounded by family having suffered a stroke that destroyed most of his brain.

My uncle was an amazing man; he lived life to the fullest. He had a kind word for everyone and, much like myself, couldn't care a less what anyone thought of him. He smoked, he drank, and partied like a rock star for all of his 72 years. A few hours after he died, when we were making the arrangements and trying to think of what to say, I remembered a quote from Hunter S. Thompson;

"Life should not be a journey to the grave with the intention of arriving safely in a pretty and well-preserved body, but rather to skid in broadside in a cloud of smoke, thoroughly used up, totally worn out, and loudly proclaiming "Wow! What a Ride!"

For good or for ill, this became my new mantra. I just turned 47. I knew I was diabetic. I had suffered 2 heart attacks. I have obsessive compulsive disorder and a degenerative spinal disease. I hit the genetic jackpot.

For more than a decade, I lived in fear. Fear of another cardiac episode. Fear of renal failure. In 2006 my neurologist told me to expect to be in a wheelchair in 5 years, and yet, I'm still dancing! A few years previous, I took responsibility for my health. I started making healthier choices, lost 150 plus pounds, and became more active. As my body changed and became increasingly healthier, so did my spirit.

At that point, I decided to love my life! I took pictures of everything and blew up my social media with moments and memories. I started documenting my journey. I told the people in my tribe how much I love them. I did things I was previously scared to do. I decided that my life story was going to be the best it could be. "In for a penny, in for a pound", nothing was off-limits, nothing was taboo. I love the rush that adventure provides, and there were times when I may not have thought things through before, enthusiastically, jumping in. I've also never been a person to do things by half-measures. So, truth be told, some of my decisions worked out much better than others.

I tried sushi for the first time and, to my surprise, I didn't hate it. Crowds were always a challenge for me, but I went to concerts and parties. I pushed through the anxiety and was rewarded with newfound confidence. I made a point of celebrating every triumph my friends experienced. I became everyone's cheerleader.

Remaining heavily involved with Dare to Share, I launched my own Dare to Be Queer in March. DTBQ was aimed at building the local LGBTQ2+ community within the larger community. I found my calling building community through the art of storytelling. I am so happy to have a friend and "spirit animal" like Diana. She supported and encouraged me in ways that I never expected, and I remain forever grateful. I am also fortunate that I have a husband who supports me to move towards my goals. I have the most wonderful, supportive employers and a job that affords me the mental space to take on projects throughout the year. In my mind, the stars aligned allowing me to move forward. I dove in head first and I still haven't looked back.

The feedback was amazing!! Not only for DTBQ, but for the involvement I had with Dare to Share. I started to recognize my gifts and strengths. I witnessed and felt the connection and healing in others. I always loved connecting with people, bringing them together and sharing resources; it was through the tool of storytelling that I discovered how sharing makes people feel less alone in their journeys. It was magical.

While this side of my life was coming together in the most meaningful of ways, my marriage was moving through a difficult stage. My husband, John, grew up in a home filled with violence and abuse, and to this day, experiences the trauma of his childhood. Over a 3-year period, he experienced flashbacks, PTSD episodes and fell into a deep depression. Drinking provided him with some comfort, and I notice that he began drinking at home more than usual. I felt I was moving forward, blossoming and coming into my own, and that John was experiencing the opposite feeling somewhat frustrated within a slower healing process.

Both of us felt we were losing each other more and more every day. He asked me to spend more time at home with him when all I wanted was to be "out there." Being the kind-hearted man John is, he celebrated my personal triumphs and successes. I loved him for this, but I felt I was being pulled down within his struggle with pain and sadness. I was thriving within my, consistent, euphoric state, yet, I was frustrated with never knowing how John would feel when I came home. Would he be happy, sad or angry?

This all became a bit of a vicious cycle, and we became stuck in a dysfunctional dance. He wanted to spend time with me because my presence felt supportive, but I'll admit, I felt his pain and sadness brought me down so, I began spending more and more time away from home.

Something shifted within me as I went into an emotional survival mode. Unknowingly at the time, my moral compass began to falter as I found myself beginning to make decisions that lacked the integrity I had always been so proud of in the past. I became self-absorbed and even made jokes about it with my friends.

Although John and I are best friends, I felt like our marriage was disappearing. We lost intimacy and connection as he focused on his healing through personal retreat and I threw myself out into the world of personal evolution. I felt powerless to do anything about it. I saw a counsellor, and he saw a counsellor, but I grew tired of talking about my feelings and hearing about his. Nothing was moving forward within our relationship. Nothing was changing, and I became incredibly sad.

Although I had tremendous compassion for my husband, I was burning out. I was so tired of living in the past, in his past. I cringed when one of his family members called him on his phone. A tragedy had befallen his extended family members, a terrible drama of epic proportions. I knew it would only result in more pain and sadness. At that time, this was John's journey, and mine was the exact opposite as I was filled with joy and adventure. We both needed to be present in our own experience but, we were being pulled in different directions.

Things shifted somewhat when I began to experience more loss; two important people in the same month. My best friend from my teenage years succumbed to a long, arduous battle with ALS. Lou Gehrig's disease stole even the most basic joy from his life. My first boyfriend passed away from kidney failure shortly after. I felt mortality breathing down my neck. Not only had I come head to head with my own brushes with death, but age and health were creeping up on me.

The previous year, John and I purchased a home in the community we both loved. John wanted us to buy a house as opposed to the condo I wanted. He vowed he would be happier if we just owned a house. It didn't make him happy, and it made me deeply unhappy. I felt the weight of even greater responsibility, and this was something I hadn't signed up for. I felt isolated and this intensified my resentment towards John. My losses continued with two more family deaths, this time on my Mother's side.

From the outside, my life looked perfect. To be fair, in a lot of ways it was. I was moving and shaking in the community! Between my job, my events, my Social Media Contracts, Dare to Share and my volunteer work, I was filling my days with meaningful work, and my calendar was always full. I even hung out with celebrities. I had an amazing support system and a network of deeply caring friends that I still hold dear to my heart. Looking back, I realize now that I was filling my life up with social engagements in order to avoid working on what was lacking in my marriage. Everything that was going wrong in my life felt too overwhelming to deal with so, I ignored it all and moved away from doing what I knew was right.

I started bonding with my good friend over our failing marriages. To respect his privacy, I will call him "Kevin." He and his wife were married about as long as me and John. I felt he espoused the same kind of intimacy issues that I was struggling with. We spent months texting until the wee hours every night to fill the void of feeling lonely and alone. We were close friends to begin with but, we began to grow even closer. In April, I became unleashed for a couple of weeks when my husband went out of town.

One night after work, Kevin came over for drinks. It was one of those warm, perfect spring nights on the West Coast. After a few drinks, we decided to get in the hot tub. More drinks inspired a very emotional conversation as we shared how purposeful we felt supporting the family whose son had passed away tragically months before. We expressed deep love and admiration for each other. And then it happened, we became intimate and spent the night together.

This encounter was not out of bounds of my marriage because of a certain agreement John and I had established many years ago. Within the agreement I have with my husband over the last 22 years, outside intimacy is not prohibited. However, we had a few rules:

- Don't ask, don't tell;
- Make sure it doesn't become a problem;
- Don't sleep with friends or anyone within our inner circle;
- And don't fall in love.

In the end, I broke every one of these rules and compromised my integrity within the commitments I had made with my husband.

I'm not sure of what, if any, agreements Kevin had with his wife, and I felt it was none of my business; we were both grown men, and we could make our own decisions. But, guilt began to creep in, and things became awkward for us over the next couple of weeks. We still had our late-night chats, however, we talked about everything but our first intimate encounter; it became the elephant in the room so, I confronted him. We were good friends before and I didn't want this to change anything. It was then that he told me he left his wife.

The guilt that crept up within me became full-blown. He assured me it had nothing to do with me or the night we spent together. I knew he was unhappy in his marriage, but I did not expect this. When John got home, I told him about our experience. He was alarmed at first because I broke the rules. Although I owned that, he quickly got over it and was somewhat amused about the experience. He was unsurprised that our close friendship lead to our night together. I told him it would never happen again, and I truly believed it. Little did I know that my integrity would soon be compromised once again as I continued trying to fill my emotional void.

Kevin was now single, and the adventures truly began. Summer was coming, and we were going to celebrate. And, celebrate we did! We grew even closer and spent more time together. He stayed more than a few nights at my home in between my family and friends who came and went all summer long. My parents showed up for a couple of weeks in July. It was devastating for me to see how much my mother had deteriorated in the months since I last saw her in February. Alzheimer's affects everyone differently, and for the first time my mother struggled to recognize me. She recognized my voice, but had a difficult time connecting with the nearly 50-year-old man standing in front of her. She got lost coming out of the bathroom in my 1200 square foot home. She claimed she wasn't hungry but, then ate everything I put in front of her. I was heartbroken and struggled to accept her 'new normal.'

My dad is a trooper, always with one foot in front of the other. He did all the right things, doctors, support groups, home care. But, at the end of the day, he was losing his wife and best friend of 50 years one piece at a time. He was grieving, and it was heart-wrenching for me to witness. As a result, my need for fun grew almost pathological, and I wasn't going to let this life pass without making a mark by making a difference. I filled my time with everything I could and avoided addressing my sadness. Instead of diving into introspection and processing my emotions, I avoided them and just carried on.

In August, I decided to go to a concert in Vancouver with a

few friends, including Kevin. At the last moment, John needed to back out. The five of us piled into my Jeep and crammed an entire summer's worth of adventures into one day. We met and connected with so many interesting characters that day and shared stories of our trip for days on social media. When all the excitement passed, my affair with Kevin renewed itself in the quiet hours of our hotel room. We returned to our homes in Parksville completely spent. Exhausted. It was so worth it but, my hypocrisy loomed over me with the guilt I felt with John.

People started asking questions about me and Kevin. Knowing I have a hard time lying, and having almost no poker-face, we agreed to let people think what they wanted but, not confirming anything. I said we were friends and when pressed, told them I didn't want to talk about it and it was nobody's business but ours. It was true enough, and I rationalized it as being within my scope of integrity at the time. I joked that we were 'keeping it casual.' Even though there was a continuous nagging uncomfortableness within me, I pushed it aside because I was having fun, and that was all that seemed to matter at the time.

John still met with his counsellor, and I attended a few sessions with him in an attempt to gain perspective on how I could cope with his state of mind. I saw a counsellor as well because, amidst everything going on, I still loved him. I wanted things to work out, but I was bereft because I felt like he was lost, and I didn't know how to fix things. I believed that he was the problem and I refused to think I could be doing anything wrong.

"In the end, I chose to manage our situation much like everything else in my life at the time as I ignored anything negative and charged full steam ahead with my newfound zest for life."

I met the most amazing people at the Dare to Share events but, I realized that my spirit was lacking. As much as Dare to Share fed my soul, there was something missing. I started doing yoga. I had never tried it before, and I was riddled with fear. From a physical standpoint, I was worried about my spine, terrified that if I bent or twisted the wrong way, I would do serious damage. I felt more confident once I got a tentative green-light from my doctor. From the emotional side, I didn't know what to expect; I really didn't know anything including the poses or the etiquette. What if someone laughed at my attempt at a sun salutation? Oh my God! My anxiety reared its ugly head. I thought this might be the perfect time to bring John into my new world. Because he practised yoga in the past and was no stranger to it, I asked him to go with me for support. I desperately didn't want to go alone. He agreed to go with me to my sister-in-law's yoga studio.

When the moment came to go to yoga, John was unable to go. Later he would tell me that being around others was draining and uncomfortable for him. He didn't have even have the strength to leave the home. His depression and social withdrawal made my hopes for connecting with him vanish. He needed time to connect with himself while I needed time to connect with others. We were at another impasse whereby neither of us was able to support the other.

I expressed my fear of going to yoga alone to Kevin and asked him to join me. He chuckled and said, "Of course!" With him by my side, I found the confidence to face my fear, and I loved it! I found the most amazing, supportive people at yoga. All my trepidation and the stories I created in my head were unfounded. The instructors were incredibly supportive and helped me with bolsters and blocks when I was struggling. Yoga agreed with me and remains an integral part of my life.

In addition to our outings and weekend adventures, Kevin and I soon established a routine a few times a week; late-breakfast or early lunch and then yoga. Then, one night in October, we planned to go to Victoria, get a hotel room for a night and visit friends. There was a Halloween party and drag show at the gay bar. Yes, "the" gay bar because there is only one. I grew more and more detached from John and began planning my exit strategy from my marriage. My relationship with Kevin while still being with John, created guilt within me and I felt like I needed to leave John in order to do the right thing for everyone involved. But, maybe not.... My soul was calling me but, my mind was chaotic; I was torn and still processing between what was right and what was wrong.

We had a fantastic evening out, then checked into the hotel and started making plans. We texted our friends to let them know we arrived and were waiting for them. I performed one of my usual 80's fashion montages, trying on 5 different outfits and ending up wearing the first one. I was so excited to share a night out in the "big" city with friends we hadn't seen in months.

We headed out to the bar and danced and partied all night! The music was fun, the costumes were incredible, and we got to see all of our friends. Kevin and I were kind of an open secret with our crowd, and no one talked about it. But during the night as we snuggled into a corner of the bar, other people we knew arrived and approached the two of us. The girls later confronted me. "How long has this been going on?" "Does John know?" "What about his wife?" I was completely unprepared and, tried to shut it down to avoid facing my part in the deception I was living. I didn't want to talk about it. As glad as I was to see them, and within self-protection, I decided it was none of their business and I didn't want to discuss it.

One of them looked at me, with conflicting emotions on her face and said, "Please just tell me this started after he left his wife." I couldn't answer. For the first time since our relationship began, other people started to factor into the equation. That guilt I was ignoring was persistently creeping in.

We got back to the hotel room and started settling in for the night. As we reminisced about our evening, I told him about the confrontation. He poured a couple of scotches, sat on the bed and told me I did the right thing. But it didn't feel right; my conscience was calling me again, and I told him I didn't think we were fooling anybody and we couldn't go on like this forever. He looked me in the eyes and we talked for hours about our ideal future.

"He just left his marriage, I needed to leave mine and we had all the time in the world. We discussed dreams of a life we could have together as lovers and business partners in exciting new projects. I called the front desk and told them we would need another night."

John started texting me in the morning. "When are you coming home?" "Can we go to a movie?" "Where are you?" "Are you on your way?" The gravity of our night was still sinking in. We decided to head home late that afternoon. He had family commitments and so did I. We drove home giggling like two kids. We had such an incredible night; here he was, the friend and soulmate I wanted. I asked for and received the connection and adventure I thought my soul was craving.

I intensified my exit strategy. I had a real estate agent do a walk through. Mentally, I started dividing up the assets and debts while figuring out what we would each walk away with. I had a plan to call John's sister and his best friend so, they could help pick up the pieces when I left the marriage. It was going to happen. Kevin and I started some business contracts and planned events together. We had a plan to make a documentary and connect with people on our way to Mexico. It was going to happen. I fully let him into my world and, we were together all the time. We met with people, had business meetings, created logos and looked into registering and trademarking it all.

One night after an event I was emceeing, John said something jokingly about the event that really triggered me. He went to bed, and I called Kevin in tears. I was a mess. I debriefed my night with him on the phone. All the emotions of the night caught up with me, and John's comment created a sadness within me. It supported me in justifying that this was the final nail in the coffin as far as I was concerned. I truly felt that John and I were done. I couldn't do this one more day. Kevin talked me off the ledge and invited me to spend the next night or two with him.

The next night I walked into his house, grateful to be somewhere serene. I dropped my stuff in the bedroom, changed into some pajamas and sat down beside him in front of the television. He listened to my story of the night before and, I cried on and off for hours. We began planning more of the future, revisiting our conversation in Victoria and eventually I cried myself to sleep. Kevin got up early and made us breakfast and coffee. John sent me messages, and I shared them with Kevin and told him I was going home to deal with the situation.

When I got back to Parksville, John was at work. I popped by and told him I would like to talk with him when I got home from work that night. John was equally upset and wanted the conversation. And so, the talking began. I suggested separate relationships and, told him that ours needed to change. I didn't feel married anymore. My life and his were headed in different directions. I had plans that didn't include him. We both cried a lot. And then, John vowed, right then and there, to quit drinking. He told me he was doing it for the marriage. I told him to do it for himself; I didn't want him to do anything for me. I was surprised at this new variable in the situation. I didn't realize it at the time, but this was a game-changer. I wasn't sure if I believed him, but I was hoping for the best.

John's sobriety was a new thing. Sober John was amazing. I was still committed to balancing my work and social life but, he seemed more present within our life together. He was fully aware of my comings and goings and, he began asking tough questions. "What are we?" "Will we make it?" I didn't trust anything at this point. He was struggling, I was struggling. In the back of my mind, my exit strategy was still moving forward full steam ahead.

My sister-in-law confronted me. Kevin and I were hardly discreet and, she'd seen us together at yoga and in many venues about town. Her suspicions were confirmed by a mutual friend and, her only concern was her brother. I didn't realize it at the time, but she became one of my rocks during this mess while also supporting her brother.

Kevin began spending more time with one of our inner circle mutual friends. I began to hear rumours they were being intimate together. Again, I didn't expect monogamy, in fact, we talked about that at length. However, he became busy during times we normally spent together, and I believed he was lying to me. I confronted him about his vow of honesty, but he refused to talk about it. I now realize the irony of my perception of his trustworthiness given my own duplicity. At the time, I viewed Kevin's behavior and mine as very different.

Feeling confused and trying to make sense of his sudden shift in behaviour, I reached out to those close to me. Something incredible happened when I shared my story with my tribe as they opened their hearts and shared their similar experiences with the same person I had been planning my future with. My storyline didn't seem much different from theirs!! I didn't want to believe what I heard. This was my best friend; surely, I was different!

For some reason, I never said anything to him, and then one night, in yet another hotel room in Tofino, BC, everything changed. After all our time together, he did something that cut so deep it took me months to recover from and I need not share it here. This was beyond anything I expected, and I knew in that moment there was no changing his mind as he asked me not to question and just accept it. As much as I needed to understand where all this came from, he made it quite clear that he was unwilling to have that conversation.

We were committed to a lot of projects and public appearances and, initially, I tried to maintain a friendship with him and keep up appearances. That didn't last long because within all my confusion, I became increasingly resentful and stone-walled. Finally, just before Christmas after a night out with friends I came home absolutely bereft and shattered with John waiting for me. He asked me straight up where he and I were at with our relationship. I told him I didn't think we were going to make it.

John encouraged me to open up about what was going on, and he promised to do nothing but listen and bear witness. I was so shattered and mixed up that I felt I was at the end of my rope; I confessed everything to John. He held me as a cried myself to sleep. Much later, we discussed how he really felt about the things I shared with him, but, at the time, the only thing he, humbly, said to me was, "Okay, let's get you through this." He placed his ego aside and showed me that his only intention was always to love and support me.

Kevin and I had made such big plans and put so many wheels in motion. We committed to businesses that required hours of contact every day. I was overwhelmed and, desperately, needed space to sort myself out. I was confused about what was right and what was wrong for me; was what I had with Kevin real, or had I jeopardized my relationship with John over something that didn't even exist? I managed to get through a broken-hearted Christmas and still worked on some projects with Kevin. We planned quite a few business meetings the following week organizing an upcoming event, and we met for lunch one day. I went with a peace offering. It was a gift that meant something to both of us. But, to my surprise, he suddenly ended everything with me with a number of beautiful reasons. I was sad and broken but ultimately, relieved. He held my hand across the table and expressed his love to me; we both agreed that we needed to sort ourselves out. At the time, I believed this came from a sincere place, and that it was one of the most beautiful conversations I ever had. We split up all the projects we were working on and said our goodbyes. Later, within what I believed at the time to be another experience of betrayal, I discovered what triggered this abrupt ending.

"I was devastated. It was beautiful. I wanted to believe everything he said to me, but, I felt fucked up and damaged and, I went home and cried in the dark for hours."

John came home, and I told him about what happened. He rubbed my back as all the tears came, and then I went to bed still confused about why Kevin had suddenly ended everything. When I woke up, I had an intuition. I still can't explain it, but something didn't feel right. I don't know what possessed me as I never, ever would think of invading John's privacy, but

I checked his phone. Not my proudest moment but, what I found was shocking! Pages and pages of communication between Kevin and my husband with John confronting him and plotting to get me out of my former lover's life. There were threats of exposure from John and denials from Kevin. I was reading them when John woke up and came into the living room. I threw his phone at him and started laughing; I was absolutely hysterical from the feeling of betrayal by both my husband and former lover. I understood it all now; this is why Kevin ended it so beautifully! Suddenly the conversation we had the previous day made sense.

I texted Kevin and told him I was aware of all that had transpired; I once again felt stonewalled. John was full of apologies and declarations of love, and I told him I understood why he did what he did and that he acted out of a place of love for me but, I was angry that he took away my choice to make my own decisions. At the same time, I finally understood that I had no perspective where Kevin was concerned. As I spat accusations at John, I realized something profound - I expected this kind of behaviour from Kevin because I had experienced so much of it during our months together but, I had never expected this from my beautiful John. Through it all, he clung desperately to me, our marriage and our family; John had been moving from a place of integrity all along, and I had not.

As much as I was starting to see the bigger picture, I was still moving through a state of anger. Both John and Kevin asked me for compassion because they both said they had no choice but to show up the way they did. However, I felt they conspired against me to achieve what they wanted, regardless of my feelings, and I felt betrayed to the core. On the other hand, how could I continue to be angry with John when he stood by me through all my acts of deception and the consequences of my actions? I was dumbfounded and began reaching out to friends, those I had not connected with over the past year. I mended friendships I ended with people I had ignored, people who didn't fit in with the new self-centered Scott. They all came back. I didn't realize it at the time but, every time I felt judged or anxious over the questions my recent behaviour raised, I opted out. Ceased contact. Ignored texts. I didn't want to hear any 'what if's.' It was becoming clear that I feared the messages my conscience was sending me.

Once the dust settled and I created distance from everything, I saw that my journey *From There to Here* was difficult to face as I realized how not in line with my integrity I had been and how ALL of the most important people in my life had acted within their integrity. All my friends, the people who I thought were being negative or judging me from their own morality, were not. They were there for me all along while looking out for me in their own way. John in particular, acted within his integrity and from a place of love. He knew I could not see the forest for the trees because of how I had been manipulated, and that my decision-making was compromised as a result. I was not responding to the chaos in my mind from my value of integrity but instead, operated from the shadows while keeping secrets and showing up as someone other than the true Scott. In the past, I was always proud that I chose an authentic way of being, priding myself on showing up as myself. But I hadn't done that in long time because I didn't have clarity about what that looked like anymore. It was killing me, my marriage and John, who loved me with all his heart.

To my surprise, John accepted a huge amount of responsibility for the place we arrived at in our relationship. He completely understood how I fell in love with this man while envisioning a new future. After 23 years together, he knows me better than I know myself. It became his mission, regardless of where we wound up in the marriage, to support my healing during this time of being shattered. John was still my husband, and he proved that he was my closest friend. I needed to prove to him that I could be my true self again within our relationship and how he sees me; a man of great integrity who does the right thing for everyone involved. I threw myself into self-healing; it became my solitary mission and responsibility. I went to counsellors and practiced yoga, breath work, shamanic healing, meditation, crystal and aromatherapy. I used every resource I could find.

It took a long time for me and John to heal both individually and together as a couple. A lot of damage was created on both sides, and we both take responsibility for our choices leading us to this place. I have thanked him so many times and begged for his forgiveness for the mess I got myself into. He just looks at me with his big brown eyes and expresses his love for me. His unconditional love is a gift but, it took me a long time to feel like I deserve it. God only knows where I would be today without his love and friendship.

Nearly 6 months later, I realize I have an amazing foundation of friends and supporters, and John and I have never been closer. He stepped up when I needed him most and deserved it the least. I was humbled, broken and now, rebuilt. I still have no concrete answers where Kevin is concerned. What were his true motivations? What did he hope to accomplish? Was I being used? I choose to take all the beautiful parts of this experience and cherish the memories, even if I can't trust that they were genuine. I truly value the transformations that occurred for me and the lessons I learned during a very formative year. In the end, my journey led me back to a place of personal integrity. It was a long and difficult road, and I would do it all again in order to land where I am today. This renewed Scott learned so much about 'who' he really is, his authentic self and what it reflects within relationships; honesty, trust and, ultimately, love. I discovered what loving and being loved really feels and looks like for me, and I know that it can change at any time. Being authentic hasn't always been easy. However, I discovered it by understanding that the choices I make affect, not only me, but everyone in my life, especially my family and friends whom I hold dear in my heart.

I DISCOVERED THE FEELING OF INTEGRITY

HOW SCOTT INSPIRES INTEGRITY

Scott De Freitas-Graff is the owner/ CEO of Extraordinary Events, an event management and planning business.

He is the organizer and master of ceremonies of Daring to Share Events, and a loyal and active supporter of Daring to Share, The Movement.

Scott believes that how he shows up in the world models a way of being that reflects true integrity with a message of caring for others, as well as, himself. He has discovered how to 'walk his talk' without preaching authenticity, but rather, simply 'being' it.

Scott is a mindful mentor as he promotes individuality by walking in his skin as a fiercely unapologetic, loud and proud gay man, who lives without the fear of judgement of others. His Dare to Be Queer events promote inclusivity as he invites all of humanity to come together in celebration of each of us being, simultaneously, unique and alike.

You can connect with Scott on Facebook at
Scott De Freitas-Graff and
Daring to Share
and by email at scottgraff250@gmail.com

INTRODUCING
JOHN DE FREITAS

I do not know anyone who moves from a place of love to the degree that John De Freitas does. He is truly the most selfless individual I ever had the pleasure of sharing a friendship with. I was once greatly moved when he took the time to meet with me to express his regret of feeling that he had not provided me with enough compassion while I was going through a difficult life situation. I was taken aback, not by his apology, but because he had supported me through my adversity and felt that his degree of compassion was not sufficient. This is who John is, a soulful, loving man, always giving to and supporting others above and beyond.

He is also a person of deep intuition, a sort of mystical man who feels everything and everyone. John, energetically, brings out the truth in those he meets; his way of being is indescribable and triggers a contagious yearning within those who enter his aura. I can't describe it any other way, except that when John enters my energy space, it shifts to an equilibrium of acceptance and peace. I know I am loved.

What is not a mystery, is that John's mandate in life is to achieve a sense of belonging as he intentionally and consistently provides this to everyone he knows.

You are about to experience John's Story of
From There to Here **and how he discovered the feeling of**
Belonging

From There to Here;

BELONGING

By John De Freitas

Belonging™

John's Story

On a flawless summer day in August of 2017, I celebrated my 49th birthday with one of the greatest adventures I could think of. As a gift to myself, I decided to skydive for the first time. From 5000 feet in the air, I took the ultimate leap of faith, strapped to an instructor with whom I placed ultimate trust. On the ground, my husband and partner of 22 years awaited with bright excitement and his camera in hand. To celebrate the day, we invited a small group of friends and family including my husband Scott's best friend, extended family members, and my mother who was here on her annual visit to Vancouver Island.

Unexpected delays with the plane's lift off didn't diminish my excitement but added to the anticipation. We enjoyed hours of laugher and conversation while surrendering to the flow of the day under cloudless skies and the August sun. When the moment arrived for our ascent, I bid my friends and family farewell and entered the plane with a supreme lightness of heart and fearlessness of the imminent experience of falling. On that day, I did indeed fall further and faster than I ever imagined. Sheer delight and indescribable emotions shot through me as I saw the earth tumble and spin beneath me. My instructor captured my experience on video throughout the dive, and I later saw myself falling again and again with the same expression of unbridled joy and surrender on my face. After landing, my entire body was vibrating, my legs were weak, and yet, I could not remember feeling so fully alive. I Looked into the smiling faces of my loved ones, and I believed that this moment on my birthday was a true reflection of where I had arrived on my life's journey.

"What I did not know in that moment, was that an even greater fall was in my future. One where I would plummet through the depths of my soul, spin through shock and fear and grief."

There would be no guide to carry me through it safely, no parachute to stop my fall, and no loved ones to wait for me upon my arrival. The image I had of myself on my birthday was a beautiful dream, and unbeknownst to me, the marriage that was the very foundation of my happiness was slipping away. For the first time in 22 years, I was about to find out what it was like to be truly alone as I faced my greatest betrayal and biggest fear. The story of my life as I knew it, was about to end.

My family history shaped my experience of what it is to be loved. My parents were immigrants to Canada, having moved from South America when I was 1 year old. My earliest memories as a child are of a small red brick apartment building in the suburbs of Montreal. I lived there with my parents, my baby sister and my maternal grandmother. At 4 years of age, I had a conscious knowing that I was loved by my mother and grandmother as they constantly showered me with affection. I did not know if I l was loved by my father but, I knew that I feared him. He was a serious man, a strict authoritarian, and his moods were unpredictable. I was often interrupted in my play and laughter with my grandmother who he resented for "spoiling me." I quickly recognized his dangerous tone of voice that demanded my silence.

Early in life, I experienced several moves before settling into a home in the west end of Toronto. I entered grade 1 for the third time at the age of 6. Changing schools had been fairly easy for me up to this point; I was bright, eager to learn and an exceptional reader. On the first day of school, standing on the playground with my classmates, one of the children, curious at my brown skin and curly hair asked me "What are you?" Somewhat self-conscious and yet understanding that she was referring to my heritage, I told her I was from Guyana. Wrinkling her nose, she asked, "What's that?" In that moment, I realized I was different from all these children with white faces who surrounded me. Before I arrived, they had only known their community of familiar looking families. But I was not familiar. I was "other". After my encounter with this little girl, I returned to our class and I contained within my 6-year old mind a profound new lesson.

As I look back on my childhood, I have lost or buried any memories of happiness within my family. Until high school, I existed in two parallel worlds of fear and victimization. At home, my father was a tyrant driven by his need to dominate my mother and his two children. He worked in the life insurance industry and achieved success but, continually felt devalued and exploited by white Canadian society. He, eventually, became depressed and chronically unemployed. Some of the discrimination he experienced was indeed real, and he succumbed to mental illness and paranoia. He found the only outlet for his rage within our home, and I lived in constant fear of his anger. He developed a complete distrust of the world that became further twisted with a puritanical belief in a Jehovah God. He believed the world was evil and Satan was everywhere. He could not sustain Christian principals so, he ceased to participate in his fellowship and eventually retained only a steadfast belief and excitement that his God was going to bring destruction to the world one day, and he would get to see it burn.

If my family challenged his rule over us, my father would turn to terrible physical violence. A storm. Horrific. Once, when I was 9 or 10, my mother and I sat together as she held our pet bird in her hands after it died. Seeing my mother's tears, I began to cry. My father came into the room and saw me crying. He flew into a rage and attacked me, blow after blow. After he finished, he apologized and told me that a man doesn't cry over a dead bird. I witnessed my mother and sister experiencing even greater violence that I cannot put into words.

My father had a particular brand of sadism that came through as a daily barrage of insults like regular predictions of me becoming a faggot and my sister becoming a whore. His eyes would burn with rage and the threat of violence. Other times we would have to sit in icy silence. Every day and throughout my childhood years, my mother, sister and I never knew what type of suffering was to come. We lived in a prison of hell.

At school, my "otherness" would demonstrate itself further. I was sensitive and self-conscious and felt more comfortable with girls. The boys certainly noticed my fragility and, under the mindset of so many children their age, I became easy prey. I was an outcast, too feminine, and too brown and fat, too different to be liked or trusted. I survived with daily protestations and tears. They called me faggot. They called me living piss. They tormented me every day. At the beginning of grade 6, my father decided a parent-teacher interview would be the perfect time to share the word of God. He brought a small, red hardcover book to my teacher that he believed would introduce true spiritual values to the classroom.

Though I had barely seen the contents of this book, somehow knowledge of it became widespread among my classmates. I remain appalled at my teacher, and whether any ethics existed for the privacy of children. Within the chapters of this book, rang out the perils of masturbation and homosexuality. I had no understanding of these terms, but a particularly vicious bully and most of the rest of my male peers seized on this new evidence of my queerness and tortured me with renewed determination. Now nearing the age of 50, memories of those 3 years in that school remain amongst my most painful.

When I was 13, I entered high school and began to realize I was indeed different beyond the colour of my skin. I awoke to a new self over the summer and blossomed with the beautiful self-confidence of a maturing youth. I realized that playing victim to the bullying was only fueling my classmates' cruelty. I ignored them and embraced new friendships and new beginnings with older students. I discovered gifts in singing and musical performance, and I surprised my peers by being the only one in my grade to be accepted into the annual school show. Soon I recognized my longing for the love and friendship of male friends was far deeper than I realized. I was attracted to men. By the time I reached 14, I knew what it meant to be gay and "other" once more.

I was taught that there was no place in God's kingdom for my gayness. Jehovah God was an ominous presence in the sky looking down on me, and his judgement of death was clear. I was certainly not going to be accepted by my parents. I lived with confusion and shame and questioned the purpose of my existence. I left home with 2 suitcases when I was 17, desperate to escape the tyranny and constant threat of violence that had brought me to murderous thoughts towards my father. While I cared nothing for my father's opinions about my sexuality, the ultimate destiny of my eternal soul remained in doubt. What I did know, in the depths of my soul, was I could not change who I was.

I learned that most children did not experience unconditional love. They grew up in homes where love was expressed conditionally when they exhibited appropriate behaviours or met their parents' expectations of the way they should be. The love I experienced from my mother was always under the dark shadow of fear. When I was 15 years old I began reading books about love and spirituality. In stark contrast to the insanity of my home, I began to learn that it was possible to be loved in a genuine way. Within a few treasured friendships, I learned that there could be many forms of love, and perhaps one day I would experience "true love" for myself. I also learned that there was another way to understand God through one's own spiritual journey. It became my quest to reveal this mystery and a love that was truly unconditional.

For many gay men of my generation, the search for love began in nightclubs. It was here where I could, at least, meet other gay men and likely find casual sex or develop friendships; I could always make acquaintances more than happy to be drunk with me. Beyond this, I remember so many of us with desperate hopes that a lover could be found and the coveted status of "being in a relationship" would be achieved. In these places, most of us were wounded children who shared the experience of being outsiders to society. We banded together, my friends and I, all members of a unique tribe. Gay friendships were complex, often platonic but not always. A friend could become a lover, or a lover a friend. Many friends were competitors, seeking to prove their sexual currency, and some betrayed you at the first opportunity. Having chosen to disown my parents in an effort to heal from my past, a very special few constituted my only family. Finally, at the age of 24, I fell in love.

Mark and I met at work. I was in customer service and he was in the marketing department. I was introduced to him and saw him around the office, and I was somewhat in awe of his handsome looks and confident charm. Soon after I started the job, and quite unexpectedly, he invited me out to lunch. Within minutes of sitting at our table in the restaurant, it was clear what Mark's intentions were. He drew me in with his blonde hair, blue eyes, good looks and British accent, and I found myself engrossed in the perfect dream. Our mutual attraction was intense, and within weeks of dating we decided that I would move in with him. It would become the most passionate journey I ever experienced, and I believed with all of my heart that I found my soulmate. At long last I loved, and I knew what it felt like to be truly loved in return.

"I will never forget that experience of first love; the colours so vibrant, our hearts filled with ecstasy, the complete absorption in each other's embrace. I surrendered fully to the experience, discovering within myself a place I never dared to hope for."

My journey of first love was to be but a brief one. As each of us confronted our relationship fears, we played out the dysfunctional patterns of our wounding. Mark ended the relationship after 3 months. Faced with the end of the relationship, the subsequent loss of my home, and an inability to return to the job where we both worked, my world collapsed. Mark's rejection triggered all the broken places within me, and the primal rejection of my parents confronted me anew. I spiralled down into a deep depression. Unable to bear the pain, a failed attempt to end my life put me into the hospital. That desperate attempt led to the beginning of my true healing.

Through intensive group counselling and individual work with a psychiatrist, I spent the next few years putting my life back together. Medications helped me to cope after being diagnosed with anxiety and major depression. What I learned about my personal wounding and my relationship to love would set the tone for every relationship that followed. This was not an easy time searching through my healing and trying to make sense of the person I had become. In 1995, I met Scott, the man who became my best friend and lover, and eventually, my husband.

Scott and I left Toronto on a stormy winter day in November. We took very little with us other than dreams of a better life. We decided to move to Vancouver, a place where Scott lived before and had found great happiness. We drove across the country and encountered numerous adventures fraught with peril. During our very first night in Thunder Bay, we were charged by a moose as we rounded a snowy cliff causing us a near death experience. The starter in the car refused to work throughout our trek, trapping us in the mountains. Our last night travelling found us settling into a small hotel in Golden, British Columbia where the fresh snow had transformed everything into a picturesque Christmas town.

Arriving in Vancouver on November 23rd, 1995, I noticed that everything was green and lush, and I was entranced to see the mountains and ocean for the first time. We rented a basement suite apartment in an eclectic community of East Vancouver near Commercial Drive. It was rich with families and diverse cultures and home to the best Italian Coffee! Scott reconnected with some long-time friends, and we settled fairly quickly into the community. Our friend Caroline had a 3-month old son, and his irrepressible nature was an instant source of joy and amusement. Today he remains a part of our extended family, a group of friends we grew to cherish. I remember those early years with a great deal of fondness and nostalgia.

The early years of our relationship were a bit tumultuous and unpredictable. Regardless, Scott and I seemed to possess a unique resilience that allowed us to weather all of life's currents, the changes and sudden misfortunes. Nine years later when Canada's laws changed, we got married. I will never forget our wedding day. We debated timing once we decided to make this commitment, and as I looked at the calendar, I noticed the upcoming Spring Equinox and had a revelation. We absolutely had to be married on March 20th; It was the first day of spring. It was auspicious; a beautiful blessing of our marriage that assured us great happiness. On our anniversary, we would always be reminded of the springtime of life and new beginnings. Scott, and I love him for this, totally agreed. We had 3 days, and our first priority was to purchase the wedding rings.

We decided we did not need or want an elaborate wedding

so, we held a small gathering in the home of a dear friend. As a gift, she provided the catering services through her business, as well as the stage for the wedding. She lined the sidewalk leading to her house with tea lights in paper bag lanterns. The evening was magical in every way. The ceremony was held on the candlelit deck. When the marriage commissioner pronounced us married, I had tears, and could see them in the loving eyes of all those around me.

Something changed in me after we married. We became something new; achieved a hard- won victory for gay rights everywhere. We were part of a movement for equality for everyone wanting the freedom to love who they chose, regardless of gender. We reached a major milestone together, and we also proved that we held each other's hearts as the closest of kin. Any doubts that may have come up over the course of our relationship to this point quickly disappeared, and I found myself in celebration of our new societal status. In truth, my love grew for my husband in profound ways. It was a new renaissance within our relationship, and over time we shared even greater dreams, dreams of a life away from the city. We had fallen in love with Parksville, where we spent so many vacations and moments rejuvenating and dreaming on the beach. Over time, we realized our dream and moved to Vancouver Island. This began a new journey together as it became the place we would truly call home.

Purchasing our first house in 2016 was yet another milestone. We had been together for over 20 years. This was the realization of all the things we were manifesting together. Scott and I were very happy within our jobs, and we loved the community of Parksville. Everything seemed perfect. But beneath the surface, problems stirred. I was working with a trauma counsellor for a few years as I attempted to deal with underlying issues surrounding intimacy. New memories resurfaced with darker demons and body memories of terrible traumas I experienced when I was 4 years old.

"I descended into a deep depression, and this did not bode well for my relationship with my husband as I pulled away into my own oblivion. I retreated from even the most basic rituals of affection and lost any connection to the intimacy we once had."

Not coping, I spiralled into alcohol abuse, emotional escape, and I withdrew from the world. I functioned outwardly, but on the inside, I struggled to contain the maelstrom of emotions. I declined Scott's numerous invitations to social gatherings. Outside myself, I observed my beautiful husband becoming ever more outgoing and social as he expanded his network of friends. It seemed a new spawning of independence for him, and who was I to hold him back? I encouraged him to be adventuresome and make new friends. I imagined that I could carry my personal pain alone and trusted that the strength of our marriage would carry us through this evolving chapter in our lives.

However, in November of 2017, Scott and I met at an impasse. I felt he was spending more quality time with his friends than me. He reassured me but, maintained an ever-changing social schedule that often excluded me. Tensions intensified, and we had a frank discussion of the status of our marriage. To my surprise, my husband began to remind me of the open terms we agreed upon when we committed to our relationship back in 1995. For many it would seem apparent that a marriage is sacred and outside sex is out of the question. For others, and most gay men, the boundaries of gay relationships are very different, and over time, absolute monogamy is rare. In the early years of our relationship we established our own rules. Don't ask, don't tell. Make sure it doesn't become a problem. Don't sleep with friends or anyone within our inner circle. And, above all, don't fall in love.

I wasn't clear on what Scott was suggesting, but for the first time, I was aware that he was seriously unhappy with the status of our relationship. Sobered by this discussion, I made a commitment that I would stop drinking entirely for 30 days, and we would review the experience together at the end of that time. Scott was visibly surprised but, agreed that we would work on the relationship as long as I allowed him to meet his physical needs elsewhere. Within a couple of days, he went out of town to do so.

I truly knew what pain was while I sat alone in my home for those two days. I was completely heartbroken and overcome by grief. My world collapsed as I felt my marriage and relationship of 22 years was about to end. All our history. All our memories. My soulmate Scott. My dear heart and best friend. Finally, I saw the consequences of my complacency and ignorance. For the last few years, I foolishly allowed my personal demons to cause me to withdraw from our relationship and take my husband's needs for granted. I was now paying the price. Dear God, sweet heaven, will you give me one last chance? Will you give me the strength to win back what we lost together? Deep in my grief, I prayed, and offered whatever price to win back my marriage, to heal the damage and, once again, share the deep spiritual love my husband and I discovered together. Nothing else mattered to me. Not our possessions or the house. None of the petty disagreements. Only the sacred bond and love between us that was beyond all barriers. Throughout this dark night of the soul, I remained completely sober.

When my husband returned home from his trip, he

reassured me that he was still invested in the marriage, but admitted he had his own personal struggles that he did not want to bring into our relationship and cause further stress for me. I was puzzled, but knowing the fragile state of the relationship, I only wanted to meet my husband at his level. I knew I needed to prove my commitment to sobriety and to the relationship, and I was willing to do anything to achieve this. Onward, through countless days, I drank tea religiously and wrote x's on the calendar for each day that passed without alcohol.

On Sunday, December 17th Scott came home from an evening out having a few drinks. He honoured our rule of having no alcohol in the house. I greeted him and sensed a deep sadness within him. Asking him to talk with me, we sat at our kitchen table. I asked him how he was feeling about our marriage. In visible pain, he told me he did not think he could share his thoughts. I pleaded with him, "How do you feel about us?" The words he uttered next carried a chill through my soul I will never forget. "I don't think we're going to make it," he said. And, he broke down into sobs and told me everything.

My husband had an affair. The individual was his closest friend, a colleague he worked with, someone he was in business with and a friend within our inner circle. At that moment, everything became clear. This very friend had been a part of our lives for years and had even shared precious moments 4 months prior as he cheered me on during my momentous birthday skydive. As the pieces fell together I did not experience outrage. Their intimate friendship and attraction all made sense, and I realized that my husband had fallen in love. At long last I had clarity about my role in this. Yes, he had broken all the rules, but I finally understood everything.

The ending of the affair broke my husband down to the

core. Stricken, but incapable of holding back the torrent of his emotions, he disclosed to me the history of the affair. He shared all the details, every moment, the ultimate heartbreak and the betrayal. He begged for my forgiveness as he could not contain this secret any longer. He struggled greatly knowing that hearing the details of his anguish would cause me more pain. But we continued this conversation both knowing that this sharing was necessary for our healing.

The affair was over. I could not judge my husband, and I knew that the karma of our relationship led to the consequences in which we found ourselves. More than this, my husband was in grave despair and grief. As I processed the most impossible of emotions, I understood that Scott experienced even greater distress than I. My instinct to console him in his pain overtook my own reactions. I understood something in the grander scheme of things. My husband needed me. I needed to protect the relationship. This was my moment and my duty, to demonstrate the true love we shared, beyond the choices we both made. And most importantly, Scott's experience was not entirely about me; it was about his own journey.

Amidst sobs, Scott begged me not to retaliate. I cautiously agreed. In order to hear his full confession, I would have agreed to anything. But as the story was told and all the pieces unravelled, I became convinced that something had changed in the relationship and Scott was being manipulated. I kept my silence for many weeks as Scott assured me he would right the situation with his friend who had reach to every corner of our lives, even our finances.

I soon realized that Scott could not accomplish this near impossible task. I found myself trying to support Scott's autonomy, but I was keenly aware that he could not, emotionally, cope with the situation. Business commitments had been made with his friend. We were tied to this individual, and a resolution seemed unlikely. I saw the pain and uncertainty Scott was experiencing; he could not follow through on our agreement to terminate the business relations they had together. We both felt like we were held hostage to the unknown.

Then, one fateful day, I experienced healing with a local shamanic practitioner. The session was a gift from my husband. Hours afterwards, I found myself in a fugue-like state. Desperate to fix our terrible dilemma, and out of passion and the frenetic energy found in my healing, I wrote a Facebook message to my husband's ex-lover.

"My only thought was to fight! Fight for my marriage and my love and the very foundations of my life! I intended only to express myself on the page but found myself observing my actions as an outsider while I hit the send button".

Despite all of my personal values and agreement to my husband, I sent a message that was a clear betrayal to Scott. I advised the ex-lover of my full awareness and threatened complete exposure of the affair if he did not terminate the personal and business relationship with my husband. I threatened his reputation and his well-being. I accused him of being a narcissist and a sociopath. I told him that unless he terminated his friendship and business relationship with my husband, I would burn his life to the ground. I told myself I was trying to protect my husband and save our marriage, but deep within I knew what I had done was wrong. Under the extreme duress, I allowed my ego's drive for survival to take over in place of compassion.

The ex-lover responded with apologies and protestations that he was not the character I painted him out to be. He told me he had vital information to give me and asked to meet with me. I saw his response as an opportunity to confront the man who had betrayed my friendship and to determine his motives. Through my own spiritual belief, I understood the soul relationship he and my husband had experienced. I even thought there was a chance to work things out for all of our best interests, to agree to see my husband resolve the friendship with a new understanding. But, my ego urged absolutely no mercy in removing this man from our lives and saving everything I held dear. In the end, he chose to not meet with me and terminated all relations and business contracts, leaving my husband with sad farewells. Scott, not knowing what I had done, came home that day and cried in my arms as he told me that the friendship was over.

I experienced something unlike anything before on that fateful night. As I held Scott sobbing in my arms, he told me of the ending that had ensued, the ending that unbeknownst to him, I had forced into being. I made a decision to deceive my husband for the greater good, for him and for our relationship. But this hollow victory was a wound beyond measure as I lied to my husband in order to save our marriage. I went against my own integrity. I took Scott's choices away. Desperate but feeling justified, I went against every principle of truth to achieve a greater good. I decided I would carry this secret to my deathbed so that Scott could be released from this toxic relationship and begin his journey of healing. I remember going to bed that night with intense grief in my heart and the dreams I had of my soul and Scott's soul in deep disappointment over what I had done. At that moment, I had lost all belonging, even to myself.

The next morning, I awoke to the sounds of my husband in shock and dismay in our living room. In attempts to make sense of the abrupt termination of his ex-lover's friendship, he went through my phone and discovered the Facebook message I had sent. And, such a day indeed! What could I say? The betrayal that had tormented me overnight was exposed in the light of day. And by the grace of God, I was devastated yet, relieved. My spirit rejoiced because I would never have to bear such a secret from my husband. But I was met with Scott's understandable outrage. I too, was outraged. Scott disregarded my privacy to discover the truth. We experienced a storm of emotion. It took us weeks to process the events that took place, but in the end, my husband understood my desperation in contacting the man who, we felt, placed our relationship in peril.

However, this was only the beginning. All of a sudden, stories of various dramas circulated within our community. There were rumours of similar relationships and circumstances involving individuals within our friends' circle. Overwhelmed and confused, questioning every truth of his experience and any truth to the stories, Scott told me he felt preyed upon, manipulated, and emotionally abused during a time when he was trying to find his way to healing. He thought Kevin was his soulmate, and although he cared deeply for his ex-lover, he felt he had been taken advantage of when he was most vulnerable. My husband experienced the revelation then, that he had been deceived by someone who could have led him through a very dangerous nightmare.

Those close to me, some of my truest friends, have difficulty understanding how I could support my husband during these most impossible of times. I can only assure them that they do not understand the whole story. I knew Scott never stopped loving me and had not given up on our marriage. Once he experienced the feeling of being manipulated, he plummeted into a deep depression that lasted for months. I have sad memories of Christmas as I held him in my arms while he shook and sobbed with grief. The whole experience left him drained of life. What my friends may not be able to understand is the heart response I had to my twin soul who was suffering and in far greater pain than me.

I could never wish to have the karma that played out for my husband. I also understood there was no way through this dark chasm unless I surrendered completely. There was nothing to resist as healing was only possible through my complete acceptance.

"My only instinct was to comfort the man I loved.
Together, in the weeks that ensued,
we began our journey to healing."

Today, Scott and I are very much on the path towards healing our relationship. We have both been transformed by this experience, and we choose to embrace each other as we work towards a new future together. I have finally landed, after the great fall, and I am slowly bringing myself to a place of trust and a hopeful future. I have rediscovered within myself, the true essence of love. I see love from so many perspectives now. I have unconditional love for a soul who is truly deserving, my husband, my dear heart and soulmate, Scott.

I am grateful for this journey that shocked me into awareness. I am so glad I rediscovered a pure and beautiful love for Scott. It has been easy to forgive, truly knowing my husband's heart. Despite the painful experiences of my childhood, perhaps because of them, I have found what I call spiritual love. It is a love for the betterment of Scott's great soul, wherever his journey takes him; Agape love as the Greeks call it. It is a selfless love.

I remain on this journey of self-discovery. I struggled my entire life for a place to belong. Not belonging in my family or with other children, and not belonging to society, I carried the weight of "otherness" for many years. However, being a person of colour and being gay, being victim and survivor, I discovered I was a member of many tribes, and to them, I do belong. Most important of all, I realized that, in our humanness, we are all one tribe and we will all experience the feeling of "otherness." My spiritual pilgrimage led me to discover the very essence of God through compassion. My belief is that the true purpose of my whole human experience is love. I needed to learn to love and receive love in return, to understand unconditional love in the divine source of my being, and to discover true belonging within.

I will hold fast to the man who has shaped the days and years of our lifetime together. Within our hearts, a fierce friendship and the fire of 2 souls have created belonging together. This is my celebration and my victory; it is the place I have landed. This is the place I will call my true home.

I DISCOVERED THE FEELING OF BELONGING

HOW JOHN INSPIRES BELONGING

John De Freitas lives in the pristine ocean-side community of Parksville, British Columbia on Vancouver Island. He has lived with his partner, Scott, for 22 years (14 years married) and he has been a proud islander for more than a decade. His family of 3 includes a shy and barky but, lovable Bichon Frise, now 10 years old. John currently works as the Assistant Guest Services Manager for an expansive luxury resort directly overlooking the white sand and some of the warmest ocean waters in all of Canada.

John, a 35-year Tarot Reader and intuitive counsellor in metaphysical traditions, is also the owner of Van Isle Mystic. His career history includes employment counselling, family support, and mental health and addictions counselling. John has worked with a rich diversity of clients and facilitated men's groups for those struggling with violence and trauma. He found passion and transformation working within the Aboriginal community and learning cultural methods for healing and personal empowerment.

John is also a passionate advocate for Storytelling and the discovery of human connectedness; he is a dedicated supporter and the Senior Executive Assistant for Daring to Share, The Event. His experience of feeling 'otherness' while moving towards a place of genuine belonging allows him a unique approach in supporting others with their own awakening, healing and transformation.

You can discover more about John at vanislemystic.com

INTRODUCING
SHAUNNA CHRISTISON

Photo by Craig Letourneau Photography

I met Shaunna in a coffee shop in Qualicum Beach, and I knew that I would cherish our friendship forever. If God needed a template of a good person, Shaunna would fit the expected mold. She is one of those people who I yearn to be around because her loving and kind energy is so contagious.

Every time I connect with her, I find myself wondering where she finds her fortitude as she, stoically, raises her triplets with her husband, and manages a career, along with all the other stuff that comes along with the speed of life.

Some might describe Shaunna as the Queen of Positivity but, she will tell you that she is just filled with immense gratitude as she uses her *Inner Purpose Feeling of Faith* to guide her.

You are about to experience Shaunna's Story of
From There to Here **and how she discovered the feeling of**
Faith   *Diana Loya*

From There to Here;

FAITH

By Shaunna Christison

Faith

™

Shaunna's Story

Looking back over my life, there are a number of impactful moments that jump out at me. There were a few momentous occasions that maintain special significance for me. One being the day I married my husband almost ten years ago. Deciding to spend the rest of my life with him has definitely changed my life for the better. I learned to love someone and be loved unconditionally in spite of our flaws, and this has been a soul changing experience for me. The birth of our three children came next. They were a surprise to us as they all came at the same time as triplets! Having these children in my life has blessed and changed me like nothing else I have ever experienced. I would be remiss not to mention how my family impacts me in the most positive of ways. Getting married and having children changed me forever, and I love to talk about and share stories about my kids. People love to hear about the privilege I feel I have been given of giving birth to and raising triplets; they are curious about this unique experience.

Apart from these significant events, there are a few others that were life changing and extremely meaningful to me. I look back and I see quiet moments that I feel may seem meaningless to others, but that greatly altered the way I see the world. They presented ever so subtly, and yet they shaped me in the most influential ways. I struggled deeply to bring myself to share my interpretations of what I experienced with others because I thought that the immense impact these moments had on me would seem irrelevant, and perhaps, un-relatable to others; the fear of judgement arose. For this reason, I found it challenging to write or speak of such quiet moments of my heart as they are difficult to describe yet, so life changing that I feel I must give it my best try.

Within the challenge of my perception of validity in sharing this story also arose the fact that it is of a spiritual nature. These experiences were shifts in my soul that shaped me into the person I am today. These moments anchor me to who I am and what I believe in. Because they are so personally significant, I am often hesitant to share them with other people.

"I have feared judgement from others. I have a faith that is alive and real to me; it is essential to me, like breathing."

In the past, I feared people will assume things about me based on the fact that I have this faith. My spiritual journey has been so deeply personal that it makes me feel vulnerable to put it out in the world in this way.

My main concern was that someone who is uncomfortable with the subject of God, religion or faith may be hurt or offended by my beliefs. But, I have reconciled that everyone has their own unique set of experiences and by sharing mine, I will not discount the beliefs of others, but perhaps inspire others to feel confident within theirs. By sharing my own story, I by no means want to imply that others should believe exactly what I do. This process of journaling these moments is personally transformative, and my intention is that my readers receive whatever they may want or need as they absorb my sharing.

It seems to me that in this particular time and culture, society has become accustomed to prioritizing physical well-being and, even to an extent, emotional and mental health. I found that these are massively important aspects of my well-being. Yet, I also found a spiritual side to me that deserves and yearns for attention and care. I moved through two impactful experiences that set the foundation for my spiritual practices today. I feel that my willingness to be open to my perception of 'God' and what is comfortable for me has been the gateway for me to truly discover what my spirituality looks and feels like. Whether I use the term God, the Divine, the Universe, or Mother Earth doesn't matter because what is important to me is expressing my experiences within my spiritual journey, rather than what I name it. I am comfortable with and will use 'God' as I share my story.

It often surprises me how dramatically these moments bubble up as they influence how I present myself as a wife and mother. Initially, I wondered how I would describe the phenomenon I experienced within them and the impact they ultimately have on the decisions I make in my life. My greatest epiphany is that they may be even more significant to me than my marriage and motherhood. At the same time, these moments changed me to my very core, and I know that I wouldn't be the wife or parent I am without their heartfelt influence. One could not have come about without the other.

I am also amazed that these two moments occurred while I was still a child. Reflecting on this taught me never to discount or discredit the spiritual capacities of my children, but rather to nurture spiritual awareness and encourage them to have a relationship with the Divine. My children are young, six years old as I write this, and I can see this happening in their lives; little indications that something is stirring deep within them, that they can't yet explain but I hope to, one day, be privy to their reflections about their spiritual experiences through their childhood.

I was a very fearful young child. During the day I never wanted to be alone, I was scared of irrational dangers. I was afraid that someone would harm or kidnap me, almost all adults were scary to me, especially men who were strangers. I had major anxiety in my early school years and within every new situation. At night, I was afraid of monsters and robbers and fires and floods and the dark and basically, any other irrational fear a child could have. I could not sleep in the dark but, had to have my bedside lamp on all night because I was so afraid.

Looking back, I wonder where this fear came from and why I remember it so strongly, so vividly. It confuses me because my childhood home was truly full of love and safety. I knew without a doubt that I was loved and I was wanted. I was a valued and important member of my family. My parents were attentive to my needs, and I remember always feeling close to both my mom and dad. There was a great deal of warmth and affection in my home for which I am incredibly grateful. I had no need to be afraid or to feel unsafe, and yet I was. Each night I was tucked in, often by both of my parents, safely and with great care for me. However, I often struggled to sleep as my anxiety took over.

"I'm not sure if this is accurate or not, but my memory is that I was awake most nights within my fear and anxiety for hours and hours."

One night after being tucked in by my parents, I lay awake in, what felt to me like, intense fear. I was six years old. For one reason or another, I was compelled to pray. This is the first memory I have of choosing to pray on my own, to reach out to someone greater than me. I have no recollection of what I said in my mind, but I know it came from my heart as I prayed. However, I do vividly remember the feeling, the sense of great peace that overtook me. It wasn't an immediate feeling of peace, but it approached gradually, like a wave that surrounded me. I was enveloped in this beautiful feeling, and with each moment it overtook me, I became more and more aware that God was somehow near me and protecting me. I was no longer afraid or anxious because I focused on this sense of God's presence in some strange and new way.

As a young child, I never thought through what I believed or didn't believe in. Clearly, I believed in God enough to turn to pray in that moment. I had no baggage with religion or societal interpretation of God. All I knew and still know is that the Divine took notice of me and was imminent in my time of fear and anxiety when I chose to turn to God. I can hardly describe how deeply this impacted me. In that moment, I knew without any doubt that God could hear me, that God heard the words I spoke in my heart or in my mind. I was overwhelmed that God took any notice of me, just a little kid and God was attentive to my thoughts and needs.

I remember crying because I was so overcome with this peace and new insight. How could it be that God was willing to take notice of me? I felt I had never done anything to deserve the love or attention of God! I was just a six-year-old girl! This became amazing Grace for me, undeserved and yet, a massive blessing to me in that moment. This was utterly incredible to me. Next, I remember feeling grateful that God would listen to me. I was thankful that my fear had subsided but that was now secondary. I was more grateful and impacted by the strong sense that I had been heard. I was in awe, and when I relive that moment I still am!

The reach of that event in my life is difficult to describe. Of course, it was my experience, and no one can take it away from me. That moment helped to shape who I am and how I see the world. I don't often have the same incredible and poignant awareness of God's presence when I pray today. It does happen, but not often.

"However, that doesn't stop me from praying and knowing that I am stillbeing heard by God at any given moment I choose to turn to God."

I do experience peace in my day to day life, and I don't struggle with fear and anxiety anymore. I feel that I am now able to rest in the love and nearness of my God, regardless of the struggles I experience in my complicated adult life while raising a family with my husband and managing a career, along with all the other things that come along.

My spirituality continued to manifest through my childhood with a second transformative moment when I was just eight years old. My family just moved from the Toronto area to Calgary, Alberta. Almost immediately, I met my very best and lifelong friend. That first summer, she and I decided to go to summer camp in the Alberta foothills of the Rocky Mountains. I had never been to summer camp before. I have great love for my family of origin, my mom, dad and older brother, and it is with fondness that I say we were truly a city-dwelling family. My mom used to joke that her idea of camping was staying in a nice hotel! While I'm sure there may have been a few, I can't recall many family vacations that included being in the outdoors and nature as a small child. So, being at summer camp for the first time, I was excited when we were told we were going on a hike. It was at this time I had another defining spiritual experience.

Walking along, even with people all around me, I was again deeply moved spiritually. I was touched by what I was seeing and experiencing in the beautiful scenery surrounding me. I can still, vividly, picture the day. It was warm, and I remember the sky most clearly; it was so open, so vast, and it seemed to me to be the most beautiful shade of blue I ever saw. The sun felt good on my skin because it was so warm and pure. As I looked up at the white fluffy clouds dispersed across the brilliant blue, I couldn't miss the towering mountains on either side of me. I had never seen the Rocky's before. I would never have imagined anything so truly huge and majestic unless I had seen them in person. I think that, especially as a child, when all things were new for me, they seemed even more exciting and magnificent. The mountains were packed densely with evergreens, and I remember feeling like the trees were incredibly bright with such a brilliant color of green. There was a little stream running beside us, and I heard it speaking to me in its own earthy language as it trickled along beside us while we walked. It was as if the whole of nature was telling me something; it was speaking to me. All the color and the sensation of the wind and the sun felt like it was trying to say something to me.

It may have been so impactful because I had never been there before or gone camping or hiking, and the scenery was truly beautiful. Yet, I once again felt so acutely aware of God, so connected to God. In that moment I wanted to fall on my face and weep. I wanted to join in with the trees and the sun and the rocks and the mountains and thank God for my very existence in that moment. I wanted to lift up my arms and jump and shout with joy for this gift I was receiving. I was moved to tears. Of course, I promptly wiped away any trace of tears so that none of my friends could see. I told no one of my feelings that day. I treasured it in my heart as my own special moment with my God. And I kept it there, hidden away for a very long time. Other than one other occasion, this is the first time I am sharing this experience. It's so personal, so precious to me, and it makes me feel vulnerable to pull it out of the deep parts of my heart.

Looking back, another aspect of what struck me so strongly was that I felt I was given a glimpse of how big God is. I could never have described it in this way at the time but, I know I was struck by the transcendence and the vastness of God; that God could be so big and yet, as I already learned, so attentive to little me. This was very powerful to my eight-year-old soul.

"It seemed to me, in that moment, that nature was telling me something about God. Not that nature was God but, that nature was revealing some aspect of who God is to me."

Nature somehow assisted me in grasping this spiritual concept, that God was interested in knowing me. Now, as an adult, it is crucial to me that I maintain the familiarity with the beauty of nature and that I don't lose the wonder. I don't want to ever stop being in awe of this incredible earth. Instead, I want to accept it as the gift it is to me, the animals and all human beings; to honor and protect it while enjoying it with awe and gratitude.

The reality of God was again impressed upon me that day. It seemed that, for some reason, God decided to reach down into my heart and let me know God was there. "Here I am Shaunna," was the whisper in the wind and in the sunshine beaming straight into my soul. It wasn't scary in any way. Instead, it made me feel that in some way God took delight in me, that I was precious to God, and for some reason, I was chosen to know God. I see and hear God everywhere now as long as I am open, and I pay attention. When I'm wrapped up in my own stuff, too busy to notice, that's when I miss my connection with God, when I take away the privilege of living this life with God in the day to day.

These two accounts of my spiritual life as a child has of course defined how I relate to God today, and they have helped to define what I believe to some extent as well. As a parent, these stories gave me a desire to instill the confidence in my children to explore their own spiritual paths so, they can live with their spiritual eyes and ears open. Ideally, I would like my children to discover God in their own way. I feel that if their awareness of God comes to them through real life experiences as it did for me, their belief in God will be deeper and more Authentic, rather than them relying on my experiences and truths.

This became evident this past year when my husband's grandmother passed away. Some family members were with her when she passed in Calgary, and I was home with my three children on Vancouver Island. When she died, my husband was at work and couldn't be reached by phone so, one of our family members who was there phoned me. They asked if they could put me on speaker phone and if I would be willing to pray. I agreed and prayed to God out loud over the phone for Granny and for the whole family to have peace and gratitude, that God would reveal God's love and compassion for the family, and they would all be bonded together in love. I was only somewhat aware of the fact that my kids were playing quietly on the floor in the living room near me.

After I finished praying for my family and for Granny, I said goodbye and that I would see them all soon, and I hung up the phone. One of my sons immediately came running up to me, red faced and clearly very excited about something. Unbeknownst to me, he had listened to the prayer. "MOM! WERE YOU TALKING TO GOD???" I regularly talk to my kids about God and about prayer so, it wasn't unusual to hear a question like this. Talking to God and prayer really are one and the same for me, and I suspected for my son as well so, I said "Yes, I was." His look of excitement shifted into full blown amazement with an outpouring of questions coming urgently and excitedly. "What did God say?! What did God sound like?! Did you call God or did God call you?! How did you know God's phone number?!" It took me a minute as I could hardly keep up with what he was asking because he was so excited. After the first or second question I realized what was happening. My son thought I was literally speaking with God on the phone, that God was on the other side of the telephone line.

I am smiling as I recount this little story about my son believing I was speaking to God on the phone because it warms my heart in a deeper way than simply being an adorable anecdote. He was six-years-old at the time, the age I was when

I had my first experience with prayer and the receiving of God's peace and the knowledge of God's attentiveness to my experiences. The reason this story touches me so deeply is that I get extremely excited about the possibility that God is reaching out to my children in a similar way to how God reached out to me as child. There are many things I want for my children. Above all, I want them to feel loved and safe and confident in who they are.

"For me, beyond the love I received from my parents within the amazing home I grew up in, these things, love and peace and confidence were all truly fulfilled as I grew spiritually, from God, not from my family of origin."

Therefore, based on my own experiences, one of the greatest gifts I believe I give my kids is preparing them for spiritual openness. I guide them in what I personally have come to believe about God but, I also encourage them to find their own paths. I believe this is done through God reaching out to them and their openness to responding with gratitude.

I have enjoyed recounting these instances in my life because I'm reminded of how real these moments were to me. As an adult, it is so easy to discount the experiences I had as a child. It's easy for me to downplay them and explain them away because now I am an adult with more experiences in the "real world". Yet when I look back on those moments, I am utterly convinced of their realness and it reconnects me to my true self. There is a spiritual side to me that deserves time and attention. I am committed to caring for my spiritual life the same way I care for myself physically or emotionally. In fact, when I neglect this part of who I am I feel so deeply unlike my true self. I realize through these reflections how my love for God must be nurtured and cared for in order for me to live my best life.

Peace is the most poignant word I can find to describe what God provides me with in my day to day life. Having what I call a friendship with God has been the greatest blessing of all for me. It doesn't guarantee that things will always go right in my life. I experience pain and disappointment the same as everyone. While life will never be perfect, I have an internal motivator to continue to grow, to bloom where I'm planted, wherever that might be. I feel lead by my faith and my God to love deeply, selflessly, and to live with integrity. I have found great joy in seeing God everywhere, in tuning in to pick up the signals from God as much as I am capable. I am convinced I will do this for the rest of my life and am committed to continue to bloom, continue to grow as a spiritual person, to be expectant for the work of God in my life and in the world and lives of others. I will always look for the beauty and goodness in all people and in all situations. I look forward to more enlightening experiences like the ones I had as a child where I feel so deeply connected to God. Instead of covering up my feelings like I did when I was a child, I want to learn to be brave enough to release them, to let the tears fall and the emotions overflow. Writing this story has been part of that transformation for me. And as I share it, I have gained more courage to just be who I truly am, a spiritual person. For that I thank you, the reader, for allowing me this great privilege, and of course the incomparable, Diana Reyers, thank you dear friend.

I DISCOVERED THE FEELING OF FAITH

HOW SHAUNNA INSPIRES FAITH

Shaunna is an Erickson International Certified Professional Coach working on Vancouver Island, British Columbia. She is working as an Authentic Leadership Global Conversation Facilitator™ and is passionate about emotional intelligence and supporting others in discovering self-awareness while leading life as their best selves. Shaunna believes that everyone's faith shows up as individually as they are unique within their presence on this earth. She encourages her clients to discover what that looks like for them while, unapologetically, living in line with her own values and beliefs.

You can discover more about Shaunna by connecting with her at shaunnachristison@gmail.com

INTRODUCING
WENDY MAH

Wendy Mah, unknowingly, supported me in facing the reality of the world of addiction. Listening to her story of recovery introduced me to the real perception of addiction, mental health and homelessness that, I admit, I used to turn a blind eye to because it scared the hell out of me.

In 2015, Wendy shared her story over conversation in a coffee shop in Kelowna, British Columbia while I recorded her experience on my phone. You see, Wendy doesn't have a computer, and she told me it would have taken her far too long to write everything down.

She lives a simple life as she takes one day at a time beginning each morning with a daily intention based on choosing one of two ways of being - doing the right thing or doing the wrong thing.

Wendy accepts her past and her lessons learned with dignity and grace. She commits to her destiny of making the right choice every minute of every day. I believe that Wendy Mah is a hero within the chaos of this world.

You are about to experience Wendy's Story of
From There to Here **and how she discovered the feeling of**
Grace   Diana Bayer

From There to Here;

GRACE

By Wendy Mah

Grace

™

Wendy's Story

I believe that I am alive today due to the grace of God. Without him, I would never have been able to be here today writing this story. It is because of this grace that I was able to find the bits of hope along the way to survive what I did. I lived most of my life as an addict, beginning at the age of 15 when one of my girlfriends got hold of some lemon gin; I was in heaven. I became pregnant at the age of 16 after seeking love and belonging outside of a family whose parents did not believe I measured up to my smarter siblings. I had a sister and brother with special needs, and my role in my family became the helper. There was much need in our family, and I often felt alone amidst the chaos of a struggling family.

I didn't do well in school and, my father's disappointment translated into my perception of not being enough. I carried this unworthiness through 4 relationships that all involved alcohol and drugs and the control and violence that went along with their and my addiction.

I was 14 when I began seeing my first boyfriend who was 21; he was the father of my child, and he was a drinker. Drinking and smoking became my thing, and I was accepted as one of the cool crowd; I liked the attention. This was the beginning of many life patterns – alcoholism, addiction, control, violence and the continuation of loneliness.

Our baby was born on September 21, 1976. He had Down Syndrome like my sister, and my parents forced me to give him away. The hole in my heart seemed to grow bigger as I became lost in self-pity and the fear of being alone. My boyfriend wanted to commit to me, and my father was furious. I vividly remember his words, "I guess I only have 2 children." I took this to mean that I was not good enough, not necessary. A whole new level of inadequacy was born in me that night as I waited for my daddy to come to my room to tell he loved me, but he did not.

My drinking escalated at the time as it enabled me to not feel. After 7 years, I broke up with the father of my child when I suddenly decided to move to northern Alberta. It was here that my drinking escalated. I worked for Canada Post, but I was an alcoholic who experienced many blackouts during this time. Loneliness and unworthiness continued to plague me.

I soon fell in love with a handsome, self-confident man. His name was David, and I told my friends I was going to marry him. I didn't know he was an addict yet, and until this point, drugs were not my thing. Then, one drink filled night I decided to try it. From there, I tried intravenous cocaine, and fell instantly in love. Nothing else seemed to matter as I became self-confident and numb at the same time. I didn't care about drinking again, and my next high was all that mattered.

It didn't take long before my guy became jealous and violent. We had weeks in between when he convinced me that he loved me wholly and completely. He asked me to marry him on a Wednesday, and we were married that Saturday. He quickly became viciously violent with me, but I believed love would cure all, and I hid the truth and blamed the abuse on myself. He was the controller, I was the victim. He convinced me to move to Vancouver to have a fresh start so, I got a transfer with Canada Post, and we got a nice apartment; life began again.

We continued with our cocaine, he drank, I worked, and he did not, ever. I soon became pregnant, and our son, Dana, was born 6 and ½ weeks early. He was just little, 4 pounds, 8 ounces, but he was perfect. I had him at the same hospital where I said goodbye to my first son 8 years earlier. I was reminded of the feelings of not being worthy or good enough. I was overcome with wanting to be a perfect mother so, I committed to being clean and sober most of the time with the occasional slip. But, as hard as I tried, my life became an exhausting and endless cycle filled with doing it all; household chores, errands and caring for my son until the sitter arrived, at which time, I would catch the bus to work the afternoon shift that ended at midnight when I took the bus home again. I would get to bed around 3 am after preparing for the next day and cleaning up after the chaos of my husband and his insanity.

David became very ill due to his drinking and drug use. His violence was unpredictable, and he could not be left with our son. I wanted to leave, but he threatened to hurt me and my family. After a while, I lost the ability to feel. He would beat me, and I just took it without crying out. His health continued to worsen, and he was diagnosed with Pancreatitis. Our marriage was basically over but, I got pregnant again. It was with great struggle that I held everything together, and then we had our beautiful daughter, Nicole.

My husband never worked so, I was basically a single mother. I worked full time while he stayed home and did opiates. It was at this time that I decided I needed help so, I took some pills. They made me feel like Super Woman and I could manage it all. I lost my job due to restructuring, and without an income, I became unnecessary so, my husband decided to let me go. I was finally free so, I packed up my kids and went to stay with my parents, dragging my addiction along with me. I used the doctors to fill prescriptions for ailments I didn't really have; the opiates made me feel moody when I was on them and anxious when I was not. My children were feeling the brunt of my shit. Their father, David died 8 years later of a massive, inoperable brain tumour.

At the age of 29, with 2 kids to love and support, I met my next man. Tim was 9 years younger than me. He was intelligent and kind, and his family welcomed my kids with open arms. He was a heavy drinker, and I continued on with my opiates and then back to I.V. cocaine. I don't remember why I started this again, and I soon felt guilty because Tim began shooting up too. We used alcohol and cocaine while the children slept.

"Our need for this began our search for heroin. I called it my 'inside overcoat' because it warmed me from the inside out."

We became heroin addicts and eventually went on the methadone program. For a period of time, we were functioning addicts engaged in family routines and activities. Then Tim had a bad fall at work.

He broke his back, and his painful recovery lead him to taking a daily cocktail of pain meds, alcohol and methadone. I, of course, joined him and this went on for 6 years. It was then that Tim's family stepped in and sent him to a detox and treatment centre. The plan was for him to get clean and then return home to take care of the kids while I went away to get clean. I missed him terribly while he was away, and I filled myself up with drugs. When he returned, it wasn't long before we were back at it and our addictions took over.

Tim went to detox and treatment 2 more times, but he regressed each time once back home with me. He became very depressed and erratic, and one March day many years ago, he came home very "messed" up. My children were out with friends and I was doing the laundry. Tim told me he wanted to get high and I knew it was a bad idea. I thought I would do the right thing and I mixed us each an injection – mine was the usual amount, and his was about 1/3 of his usual dose. Already messed up, I injected him with our poison.

I left to do the laundry one building over, and when I returned he looked like he was sleeping. But he was not; he was dead. I called 911, and the paramedics worked on Tim, but he did not survive. He was only 28 years old. I was instantly filled with fear. "How will I go on? Was I to blame?" The paramedics and police declared his death "unexplained." My next thought was "What was to happen to my family?" All my feelings of being unworthy and unnecessary came flooding back. And now I had to add murderer to my resume. I needed to not feel, and I began using heroin heavier and heavier to numb everything out.

After 5 months, I met Ray. He was from Kelowna, and

he was a single dad. We seemed to have a lot of in common, and he was extremely protective of me; in my mind, being protected meant I was worthy and safe. He was a drinker, but not an addict and he encouraged me to get my life back. Our relationship grew, and I hated being alone so, we became a family.

The children and I moved to Kelowna to be with Ray. The ministry had cut me off, and I had no income so, I thought this was a good idea. Ray was very good at words, very confident, very demanding of attention and controlling. He would walk into a room and everyone would turn around. Not that he was anything special, but he had a presence about him. I felt like we were going to be looked after by him. so, we moved into this small 2-bedroom house; he had 2 small kids, and I had my 2 pre-teens. My kids were in school and his kids were home all day so, we did everything with his children. At 3pm, he started drinking for the day, and he would say "No more kid's stuff." He meant it. That was when my kids were coming home so, not only did they lose their whole life by moving to Kelowna, they also lost me.

They, of course, began acting out in different ways. They were angry and confused because I wasn't allowed to do anything with them, and Ray's kids would tell them about all the things that I did with them. It was a very difficult situation because any time I stood up for them or myself, I was told I was wrong. If I became strong and voiced my opinion, I was told I was wrong. His drinking became completely out of control, and my role in our relationship was to support him and his kids on his terms. To do what he wanted and with him, including drinking. I needed a roof over my children's head.

He was very manipulative, and when he didn't get his way, he would just snap. I believe he suffered from some type of mental illness because he would be ok and then snap; he would love me one minute and then absolutely hate me and have the ability to kill me the next. He would love to kick me and my kids out into the middle of the street. We didn't know a soul in Kelowna, and there we were trying to find a woman's shelter or somewhere else safe for us to go to.

When Ray was 17 years old, he did his first stint in jail so, he was a hardened man. This set the tone for his life. I decided that I was going to fix him. But that was not the case. Instead we developed this pattern of him kicking us out and us coming back. We found a bigger house together, and he agreed that this would be our new beginning. Unfortunately, this didn't change his behaviour, and he continued kicking us out; his violence got worse and worse. He got physically violent in front of my children, and when he got fed up with my kids, he was abusive with them as well.

Ray wanted a mother for his kids because their biological mother wasn't around. Any time I would be a mother to them, and he was in a good mood, it was really good, but mostly, it was "Don't listen to that bitch." He taught his children that they and he were better than everyone else. Eventually, his kids took on this same mindset, and after a year and a half, I finally said "Enough." I didn't want my children to be left out in the cold any more as he continued to throw us out time and again. We ended up at the Kelowna Women's Shelter or at a house of one of a few friends I had made. He always talked us into coming back. He made me feel less than because I had no income and no money of my own; I believed I could not be on my own or take care of my kids. So, I decided to suck it up and be honest with the women at the shelter, and I asked them for my help.

We got out and left him....sort of. We moved to a safer

environment, but now I had 2 houses to clean and 2 households to cook for and do laundry for because even though we were out of his house, I didn't detach completely; I was still in a relationship with him. It amazed me and others that I would go back to Ray and try to mend fences, even those that weren't mine to mend. The reason is very simple, I didn't want to be alone. Any time I was alone, I felt the loneliness of when I was a little girl. There were many reasons why I never felt a part of my family. Many times, it was because I put myself apart from them. They needed so much help that I separated myself from them. So, as a child, I didn't spend a lot of time physically alone, but I chose to be alone in my head. As a result, 'alone' was somewhere I didn't want to be during my adult life. I wanted to belong to someone and to a family. Alcohol and drugs gave me a sense of belonging, and Ray never understood the drug part of my life. Every time he kicked me out, he accused me of doing drugs. The truth is I wasn't, until I was. I think that because he accused me of being an addict and I wanted to belong so much, my mind tricked me into believing that's who I was.

I wasn't living in the best area of town but, it was where I could afford housing in order to live on my own. There were a lot of drugs surrounding me, and I met drug dealers, addicts and users every day.

"When I'm not aware, I am a pretzel and I will mold into what is around me.
I often wonder where my head was at back then."

I started doing more and more drugs and, for lack of a better way to describe it, I lost interest in my children. Things became more difficult at home as my son, Dana became very violent and dissociative. In grade 9 he got into drugs as well.

I removed myself from the situation and got high. Although wrong, it seemed to make things better for me. I was in trouble with Ray for doing it, I was in trouble with my children for doing it, and I was in trouble with myself for doing it. But, I did it anyway.

Things went on for 2 years that way. Dana got more violent. If I asked him to start his homework, and he came after me with a butcher knife or a hammer. I was terrified, running up the stairs screaming, the neighbours calling the police. The police told me I had to charge him, but I would not. In hindsight that's what he needed, but I could not do that to him. I knew I was a big part of Dana's problem because he had anger issues and attention deficit disorder. It was my responsibility to get him the support he needed. Throughout his life, I fought with doing the right thing; I was an addict, and I didn't want to push a drug on him, even though I knew it could help him with his ADHD. I questioned whether to give him the drug, or not. I knew if I didn't, he would fall through the cracks of society in school because he couldn't focus. I had very few people to communicate that with in order to do what was right for my son. In the end, he did take medication because there was very little behavioural therapy available for him. Unfortunately, the irresponsible addict in me didn't always give my son the pills, and when I didn't, I took them. This is not an easy thing for me to admit, but this is what I did; I took my son's medication away from him and, used it myself. Maybe this is why I feared him being prescribed them in the first place, because I knew what I was capable of.

I did so much damage to this poor kid. But, I decided that I could fix it all by loving him a little bit more. That cycle never stopped. My son's violent behaviour became worse than ever, something he learned from all the wonderful men I picked;

this is how you treat women. Then one day, there was a knock on the door. The Ministry of Child and Welfare Services asked me if I thought it was fair for my daughter to be living among all this violence. Of course, I agreed that it was not fair to her. I always knew that my son's issues were not just a Dana problem, but a family problem. I got that.

The Ministry offered family counselling, and I agreed to go with my children. My daughter and I went religiously for a year, but Dana never went. By the time Dana was 16 and after many, many police incidents and reports, the Ministry knocked on my door again, and gave me an ultimatum, either Dana leaves this home, or we take Nikki away from you tomorrow. My daughter had found a bit of a voice, and perhaps she began sharing her home life at school so, someone made the decision to support and protect her. The Ministry gave me a choice that day, to either let Nikki go while having done virtually nothing wrong, or to let my son go?

It was winter time, and I made up my mind as I changed the locks one day after Dana left the house. He had been out on the streets dealing drugs, but he knew he had a place to go where he could come and be safe and warm. This time, when he came to our house, the doors were locked. I listened to him bang on the door, crying and screaming "Please mom." Another glitch in our system as my daughter is protected, but my son is out on the street with nowhere to go. I remember sitting on the other side of the door, clutching his pillow and smelling him through the fibres as he begged me to let him in. I knew that I could not open that door, and I didn't.

My son never physically hurt us again, and he lived at the Gospel Mission, a local shelter for the homeless and on the streets; he learned all the wrong things. I remember riding my bike around the city looking for him to give him sandwiches and leftover food. Was this the right thing to do? I don't know, but as a mother, it was the minimal I could do. He would always take the food and then yell obscenities at me. I was ok with this because I believe I deserved it and it validated all the bad within me and the bad person I was.

I started doing more and more and more drugs, and I hung around with people who did drugs. My daughter was 13 years old then and home alone most of the time. I lost my income and spent most of my money on drugs so, I lost the house I was renting. My daughter and I moved from one place to another and in between places, we lived in some really horrible places. Finally, she did what she had to do and went to her school and told someone she trusted, "I can't stand this. My mother is an addict, and I am not safe at home." She was taken into foster care. I have told her many times how proud I am of her for protecting herself at such a very young age.

I am grateful that my daughter was taken care of, but this provided me with even more freedom to go further and further into the drug world. I have been asked how one can go any deeper into that world than I already was. I can't answer it. I just did. The sad part is that I wasn't even close to the depths of hell I ended up in.

I got to visit my daughter, and by the time she was 15, I got her back. I went to counselling, stopped taking drugs and went on my Methadone maintenance program so, that I wasn't physically needing anything. I decided to focus on my daughter because she deserved it. Everything was going along nicely, and what do I do? I go back into the drugs. I think I did this because there was a part of me that believed that I didn't deserve all this goodness so, I self-sabotaged myself when things went well. I really believed that I was not worthy, and that I failed her before so, I'm going to do it again. I didn't believe in myself, and I didn't think I could do the work that I needed to do to be a good mom.

I still went back to Ray's off and on, and I would sneak my son in. There was tricky, tricky maneuvering all the time. I was becoming more and more dishonest, shifty and manipulative. When I was on the Methadone program I needed to provide drug screens. I would have my daughter pee in a jar and I would pour a little bit of Methadone in it, and it worked for a long, long time. I'm not proud that I asked my daughter to do this, and she didn't know the real reason she was peeing in the jar. At the time, I told her that we needed to make sure she didn't have the bad infection I had because I didn't want her to worry. When I didn't have her as cushion, I would go back to heroin. None of this went well with Ray, and he continued to take me in and kick me out.

I was not allowed to come home until Ray came to get me. Sometimes, that was a couple of days, or a week and sometimes it was a month. It was when he decided because he had all the power. He knew where to find me, and he stood across the street with his arms crossed. That was my signal to go home with him for a few days until he kicked me out again.

I know now that everything I went through, whether right or wrong, was what I needed to experience. Sometimes, I wonder if I created a space for me to be alone when I sabotaged my chances of having my daughter back with me. Maybe I needed to be alone, the one thing I feared the most. Maybe I needed to face this fear in order to move forward to being well. Maybe I needed to lose what was most precious to me to feel what it was I needed to feel. Nikki made another call; she was removed from me again.

We were living in a motel at the time, and I remember hugging and crying with her. Both very upset, I told her "You are an amazing girl, and I love you." I knew that she would succeed in her life, and I needed to let her go. I fell into a deep depression. When I saw my son, he would spit in my face. I was so desperate that I ended up back with Ray. He was always on the back-burner, and he took me in again. Of course, he hadn't changed, and he continued to control me and throw me out; the pattern continued. I had nowhere to go when he kicked me out because the only people I knew were drug people in downtown Kelowna.

"I needed money, and there are a few ways to make money out on the street. One is as a working girl, but I would not have been allowed to go that route because too many people cared about me."

I was everybody's street mom out there, and my son slowly started to see that I was not such a bad person after all. However, it was very difficult to have a mother-son relationship being in the situation we were in. We slowly became street friends; I became my son's friend within that world. This was deflating and heartbreaking for me, but, my son was finally embracing me as a human being, and I loved it. I couldn't get enough of it. Being a part of this world with my son saddened me then and it saddens me now. For years I got high with my son and I worked for him. This is the part of my story that bothers me the most. Because a mother doesn't do that. I felt protected and safe under his umbrella.

My addiction became so stupid and out of hand, and around 2006, I was arrested for the first time for either trafficking or procession, I don't remember. I was processed down on the coast in Surrey, and my girlfriend drove with me in the van. I was suffering some withdrawal, but at this point it was manageable.

I remember the devastation when I eventually landed in the cell alone. My friend was moved, and there I was, shackled, handcuffed, and alone. I was so scared, and I bawled my eyes out having visions of what jail was like and what was in store for me. I had to quickly pull myself together because I didn't want anyone to see that fearful part of me.

It turns out that jail did not mirror the visions I had. I wasn't there very long, maybe a couple of months, and it was actually ok. I detoxed in there, and once I got out, a new cycle developed. I had a parole officer who gave me specific conditions, but I would never comply with them. A judge once asked me why I would not comply, and I answered, "It doesn't matter anymore. If I'm not allowed to go downtown, I will die." What that judge likely knew is that I sold and did a lot of crack cocaine to supply my heroin addiction so, in my head, if I can't go downtown, I can't live. Even though I had just lived for 2 months in jail drug free, in the real world, I believed I couldn't live without it. At that time, that's all I wanted, to be with my people and not be alone. These were the people who got me, they understood me, they thought the same way I did, had the same thought processes I did, and they became and were my family. Some of them are still out there struggling, and some of them are in recovery, but hundreds of people called me "Mom." To feel accepted, loved, connected and to avoid being alone, I found solace out on the street with my new family and fellow drug addicts. This became my world, my comfort. This went on and on, and my last arrest was in 2012, with many in between.

There were times when I didn't have to be out on the street, but most of the time, I did, and in order to be warm and safe, I needed to be around some pretty awful things. I've seen a level of craziness on the street that is indescribable. I've seen people die and I've seen people killed. What needs to be known is that as the drug world moves up in degrees of harm and risk within its corporation, the levels of evil increase as well. Much of it is unthinkable for most and, perhaps, unnecessary for the outside world to know.

This world also presented its share of illness. I suffered from minor ailments like "street feet" that is horrifically painful and disgusting. I became inflicted with the MSRA infection, Methicillin-resistant Staphylococcus Aureus infection. I've had 12 surgeries to manage this infection; every piece of flesh is removed to the bone in order to stop it from spreading. It's highly contagious and very prevalent within the hospital system. I probably got it as often as I did because I would dress the wounds of my family on the street when they were injured. We all took care of each other.

Another time, I broke both arms and ended up with 2 casts. While riding my bike on Lawrence Avenue the light turned yellow, and in my drugged state, I thought I mustn't interrupt traffic. So, I stood up to go faster, and the hoodie I had tied to my waste fell down and got caught in my front tire. The bike spiralled forward, and when I held my arms out to break my fall, I broke both arms. Besides the pain, this presented a bigger problem. I'm a junkie so, not only were my arms broken, but my hands were also numb from the injury so, I had very little mobility. It's very difficult to shoot heroin without the use of your hands and arms.

Another time when I just didn't feel right. I was tired and pale and falling asleep everywhere. After 2 weeks, I woke up very sore around my collar bone, and it was red and inflamed; it felt like someone had beat me. I went to the hospital, and it turns out I didn't have a broken collar bone. I was sent home, and I lay in bed for 3 days in agony. Being an addict, I could only rely on my people for so much so, I had a brainiac idea that

I would get up and go to the outreach centre and get a sling for my arm. I knew that if I had a sling, I could stabilize the arm, reduce the pain, buy some dope, sell the dope, and then get the heroin I needed. This was my plan. I got to the shelter, and they were relieved to see me because the hospital was looking for me. My blood work presented with osteomyelitis, a staph infection inside the bone. What this meant was that I needed to be in bed in the hospital for 6 weeks.

The doctor who admitted me told me that I had to stay in the hospital for 6 weeks in order to recover. This would have been an opportunity for me to come clean. Did I take this opportunity? No. I looked at him and asked him, "Do you know that I'm a heroin addict?" He looked at me in complete bewilderment. I told him that I couldn't fight my addiction at the same time as fighting the infection. With all the pain I was in, I tried to get out of the chair to walk out of the room. Suddenly, he raised his voice and said, "Stop! You will surely die!" I looked up at him, and I said "I know" as I continued to move towards the door. He asked me what he could do to keep me there so, I told him that I needed a pain management regimen in order to stay. He agreed. He substituted the heroin with opiates, specifically Dilaudid. I, in turn, spit them out, and went into the bathroom to inject them; I did this around the clock for 6 weeks. I chose this method because I was just as much addicted to the ritual and the steel of the needle as I was to the actual drugs. Such a very sad state to be in, but I am not alone. I believe he knew what I was doing but, turned a blind eye to it because he knew it was a necessary evil. I was not super high, but it prevented me from being very sick through detox.

When I left the hospital, I went to a friend's house to recover further. I initially wanted to start another round of the methadone program but, realized it wouldn't work because

I was living with another heroin dealer. I started using and dealing again. My friends provided me with the drugs I needed to sell in order to get the heroin I needed. I never sold heroin, I just used it. I knew the hell that came with heroin withdrawal, and I did not wish that on my worst enemy. This doesn't make me better, but it was a line I wouldn't cross. I also knew that selling heroin would affect me financially because I would be too sympathetic to my buyers' needs, and I would end up giving a lot of the heroin away. Although, this doesn't make any sense today, in my world back then, it did.

"I didn't know how to be a mother anymore, and I thought I lost the privilege of being a mom to my son and daughter."

So, to compensate, I became a mom to the people on the street. How appropriate that my last name is Mah! One day my daughter wrote me a letter when I was in jail. She asked me, "Mom, do you know how hard it is to know that everybody out there calls you mom?" This hit me so hard because she deserved a mother and I didn't even think that I was worthy of living let alone being a mother to her. My daughter lived in foster care all those years, and eventually she "aged-out" and made a life for herself. She never took drugs or became a part of that side of my life. I am so proud of her and so grateful that she made the decisions she did. Life has not been easy for her, but she rose above it all, and she continues to make the right choices.

I got to a point when I was using ridiculous amounts of heroin. I woke up in the morning and walked to the city park washroom to shoot up incredibly high doses. From there, I would try to walk to the Gospel Mission where I knew I would be safe, around people. I had no sense of direction and I walked in circles. I could have walked right into the lake and drowned without knowing what I was doing; I was not in my head anymore. I remember seeing passers-by and asking them to walk me to the Gospel Mission for $5. Such ridiculous behaviour towards a death warrant, and it went on and on and on.

There is a parkade in downtown Kelowna, and I liked to go to the third floor of the stairwell. This is where I did my drugs, did my business and spent time alone there. One very cold night, I was doing my heroin, and suddenly, I was unable to function. I heard a voice that was urgent, but loving, saying "Wendy." I looked up and across the elevator lobby I saw my jacket and all my hoodies. I had a little tiny spaghetti strap top on, and I was freezing cold. I thought this is weird, and I went over to where my coats were. I layered some on and sat with the rest of them. Time lapsed; it could have been 10 minutes, it could have been 2 hours. What I do know is that I was blacking out. I heard that voice again, and I looked up to see my coats and hoodies on the other side of the lobby; I was sitting in my little tank top for the second time. Nothing clicked as to what was going on at the time, but I now know that I was overdosing. When one overdoses, they become very hot so, that was why I kept taking my coats off in sub-zero temperatures. Finally, after just feeling incredibly confused, I came to some of my senses and walked out because I knew that I had to get out of there and be around people; I knew I was in an unsafe state; I knew I was dying. I often wonder who that was who kept waking me up. Was it an angel? Was it God? Or was it just me wanting to live?

My last arrest was on July 11, 2012. I was sitting outside the Friendship Centre, and an officer came to me, and asked, "Is it time for us to rescue you again?" He called it a rescue, but it was an arrest, and this time it felt very different from any other time because I didn't want to do this again. Before, going to jail was like a family reunion; once I got through the withdrawals, it was easy, like a mini vacation. But it didn't feel that way this time. I had the worst withdrawals I ever experienced. I was handcuffed and shackled, and I continuously threw up green bile for hours on end. I didn't know how I was going to live without the dope. I didn't know if I wanted to live without the dope. I didn't even know how I was going to continue living anymore. I wanted to die.

I suffered greatly from the withdrawal, but once I got through the hump of it, and I was moved to ACCW, Alloette Correctional Centre for Women in Maple Ridge. Again, I noticed that it wasn't the same this time. All the gang was there, but I didn't want to socialize. I wanted to be alone which is not at all like me. Something in me had shifted. I didn't want that life anymore; I was done with it. The problem was that I didn't know how I would change that. On July 30th I talked to my lawyer, and he told me that I had a bail hearing coming up. I laughed because I knew that no judge in their right mind would ever grant me bail; I didn't have any money and I never complied with the conditions. He asked me if I had a plan. I told him I would get back to him, and I left and started to think. I remembered the women at H.O.P.E Outreach[4] who were always available to help us on the street. Angie Lohr, Kelly Lim and their team would magically appear and ask us, "What can we do for you?"

---

[4]Hope Outreach is a night-time outreach to homeless and exploited women. **H.O.P.E**. stands for **H**elping **O**ut **P**eople **E**xploited and was started in 2008 by two incredible women who wanted to be the voice for those vulnerable women who do not have one. **H.O.P.E**. operates in the small town of Kelowna, B.C. and is 100% donation funded.

"So, I phoned them, and with all the attitude in the world,
I asked them, "What can you do for me?
Here I am, I need some help now
What the fuck are you going to do for me?"

The response I got was not one that I expected, "Yes, we will go to the judge and we will speak on behalf of your recovery. Yes, we are going to help you." I phoned my lawyer and told him that I had a plan. I felt very empowered because I had never had a plan before in my life!! On July 31st I was out on bail, and on my way to the H.O.P.E recovery house.

Part of going to the house of H.O.P.E was going to meetings, and in order to go to them, one needs to be an alcoholic which of course, I was as well. What really resonated for me in those meetings was the importance of being honest, to be open and willing. At that time, I didn't know how to be honest because I had created and lived a life of lies, a life of deceit. Mostly self-deception. I started speaking my truth; it's not ok to use with your son; it's not ok to not have contact with your daughter; it's not ok to sell dope; it's not ok to live on the streets; it's not ok to think so little of yourself. I started being honest and facing the truth, and a lot of things were hard to swallow.

The first thing I had to tell them was that I had been 'chipping' or treating myself to a bit of heroin here and there. My dealer lived a block away from the recovery centre, and I was pre-wired to be an addict; not a good combination. I decided to tell them that I was using again. I said it! It was one of my bail conditions to commit to this program and be honest so, I did. I was very worried about going back to jail so, I was willing to take the chance to be honest. For the first time, I knew that I had to be in order to recover and move forward.

I asked them if I could detox at the house of H.O.P.E, because I told them that I knew I could do it. I was determined to beat this and finally start living the life I was designed to live. They allowed me to do it there, and it wasn't that bad. Then one day, they announced that I had to go to my bail supervisor and they urged me to tell her about my 2-week relapse that started with my 'chipping.' I was so angry with them because they made me go and tell the truth. The bail supervisor wrote me up and told me that I would likely need to go back in front of a judge. I thought for sure that I was going back to jail. But, I changed my mindset and thought, "I have a little better head on my shoulders, not great, but better, and I will just have to deal with the consequences." I was so lucky because my bail supervisor's supervisor signed off on it, and I received leniency.

I was then offered the Boot Camp, which is doing the 12-Step Program in 3.5 days, 7 to midnight for 3 of the days. It was so hard, but it saved my life. It inspired me to be open to seeing things differently. It opened my heart and made me see my wrongs and own them. I made most of my amends . In my past, I stepped on people who didn't deserve to be stepped on. I did a lot of bad things in my life, and I can never make them right. I do know that if I had a do-over, I would do a lot of things differently. I'm not the same person I was back then. Today, I see people I knew from that life, and when they see me, they tell me they can't believe I'm the same person. I see RCMP officers who have tears in their eyes when they see me because of all the people they thought might recover, I would have been at the bottom of the list.

I'm so grateful to everyone who has been on my journey. I am working every day. As we speak, my son is sitting in Calgary Remand with 23 hours a day lock up. He's working on his 12 Steps and he's moving through recovery. I don't like to think of him in jail, but that is our pattern and it's up to him to stop it. Today, I am a grandma, my daughter has a beautiful daughter, and I help her out as much as I can. I try to do the next right thing every day. I've done a lot of things in my life, and today it's so clear what I need to do. Some days I'm not sure, and I just sit still and wait until I get the answer. I wake up every morning, put my 2 feet on the ground, and I make a decision whether to do the right thing or the wrong thing. It's my choice.

I'm still in touch with my friends on the street, and they call me when they need help. I try to be a role model and guide them with love towards something better. I am living in the world of recovery, but my heart will always be with my family in the world of addiction. When I was out there on the street doing my thing, I still had a mom's heart. I've been through much heartache in my life, and I know that each of these lost souls are going through their own reality of pain. When I lived on the street, I spent many hours listening to them; they need someone to listen to them; they need to have a voice; they are human beings just like anyone else. They are somebody's father, son, mother, daughter. I will never, ever forget them. If I can let them be human for just one minute, then I have done one good thing in my life.

I learned about mindfulness years ago at Crossroads, otherwise known as The Bridge, a recovery centre in Kelowna, British Columbia, Canada. We did something called 'Mindful Walking' in Lions Park. I remember walking like soldiers in silence. It felt ridiculous at the time. Now, thinking back and having been through my recovery at the age of 52, I realize that it is all about being present – there is purpose in everything I do, and I have discovered what that is for me. I am consciously aware of what I'm doing and why I'm doing it.

Through all my years of addiction, I received a lot of help from many people before and after things got really bad. Whether my family, friends on the street or strangers having coffee with me, I don't think most of them even knew they were helping me with the little things they said or did. I didn't either, until all their insights came back to me years later when I was ready and needed their guidance. A lot of seeds were planted through this whole process, and in the end, that is what made recovery easier for me.

I don't believe in triggers; I wake up every morning, and I remember who I was. Even though I am still that person, I know where she can take me and that it is God who continues to support her in surviving this journey. I make a decision every day and tell myself "Not Today." Since my recovery, there have been people who have used drugs in front of me. It's not a trigger for me because I know that could be me again. Just one hit will take me back to the depths of my demise so, no I don't believe in triggers, I believe in the grace of God and the choices he provides me. It is my responsibility to be aware of them and choose what is right for me.

I DISCOVERED THE FEELING OF GRACE

HOW WENDY INSPIRES GRACE

Wendy's current focus is on her health and well-being while consciously showing up in the world as a role model for her children and grand-children. She works in a dollar store a few days a week where she enjoys the simplicity of the camaraderie of her customers.

Wendy pays her gratitude forward sharing her vast post-recovery survival skills and knowledge while supporting others working at a recovery house 4-days a week.

Wendy never understood why she wasn't seriously injured or didn't die throughout her years of addiction. She now knows that it was Grace that saved her, God's Grace. She believes she had to go through what she did in order to show others that there is hope and that the Grace of God is there waiting for them as well.

INTRODUCING
DONNA FITZGERALD

Photo by Amanda Van Order

I met Donna Fitzgerald at a trade fair in 2010, and we have been friends ever since. She has a sense of calm about her that masks all she has gone through from the rest of the world. It's not that she wants to hide her past, she has just learned how to manage it within her present to create a sense of peace as she moves through her daily life.

Donna is committed to daily journaling, a tool that continually provides her with clarity about herself; she utilizes her writing as a guide towards whatever her next decision might be.

I have never met anyone who has been dealt as much personal adversity as Donna. And yet, she perseveres through each hardship as it comes her way with the utmost grace and humility. She never presents as a victim, but instead, a pillar of strength and gratitude.

You are about to experience Donna's Story of
From There to Here **and how she discovered the feeling of**
Calm

Diane Bayer

From There to Here;

CALM

By Donna Fitzgerald

Calm

™

Donna's Story

It has taken me a long time to discover that being a victim of childhood sexual abuse brought me to a place of complete gratitude and calm. It wasn't until I arrived in my mid-fifties, that I was finally able to put the pieces together. The only reason I accomplished this feat was because I finally chose to learn how to love every piece of myself, and subsequently accept those other parts that were not easily understood. I moved through a sequence of adversity, experiencing the abuse by my father, being challenged emotionally, physically and spiritually as a caregiver to my husband who suffered from ALS for 6 years, then raising my children on my own from the onset of his illness and long after his death. I supported them financially and emotionally, at times feeling like I could not go on. But, I held on and perservered by tapping into the love and gratitude that came from a deep place within my heart and soul. I now realize that each of these overlapping periods in my life were all part of a bigger plan for me, one that was provided for me to understand who I truly am and to be comfortable with her, with me, with my unique self.

From my soul, I am the same woman I started out being so many years ago. The difference is that by learning to listen to my inner voice, I have gained clarity about who I am with all the layers of wisdom I obtained while moving through the experiences I thought would break me at the time. This has made me the same as I was, yet different because I took the time to understand who I became and how these things transformed me. That is the gift; the gratitude I fostered from all the bad stuff I was served thus far. The gift of gratitude that came from all the abuse, living in, beyond financial and emotional capacity, and being on the brink of breaking for so many years. No matter how painful it was, I am ever so grateful for having the courage to consciously decide to discover who I am and what I am destined to be and do on this earth.

My journey of self-discovery began in 2003 when I chose to be open to understanding more about myself. I was lost, burnt out and searching for Donna. This choice continues to provide me with never-ending inner evolution. I will always welcome this continuum of learning and ultimate transformation because each step takes me closer to knowing who I am from a soulful place, and more connected to the blessings in my life and that feeling of gratitude.

It has been a difficult cycle of ups and downs as I still struggle to understand why I didn't recognize who I truly am until later in my life. All those years, I really believed that I was this little victimized child who had to stay stuck in her abuse and her internal pain. Looking back, it feels like such a lie but, maybe it was the truth until I became aware that it wasn't; after all, perceptions are only true when you believe them. Now, after so many years of committing to understanding myself, new awareness has created new perceptions and truths have been unveiled. The internal pain has transitioned to internal love, and I see myself in a new light as a woman who experienced that pain but, has replaced it with self-love. I am still that little girl who was abused, but who is now healed, loved and honored by my adult self.

I began to unlock my abuse when I, simultaneously, began my journey of self-discovery. Being abused at such a young age, I locked the memories and emotions away to survive. I have yet to find clarity about why. I have retained the knowledge that the abuse happened, along with some memories, but I believe that I locked away the severity and frequency to protect the little girl within me. There is so much research and many theories about this, but I don't think it matters anymore.

"What I do know is that being abused by my father had an immense impact on the person I was and the woman I have become; more than anyone will ever know."

He was someone who was supposed to guide and support me and act as the leader and head of my family. Not only was my childhood taken away from me, but my way of being as an adult evolved into a woman and mother whose role was greatly shaped by the victim of abuse I became. I now know the abuse as a child stifled my light, and I became a shy, insecure child who always wanted to please others. It changed who I am, and my mother added to this transformation by choosing not to protect me.

It is difficult to determine what is worse, the abuse that my father bestowed upon me or the protection I was deprived of by my mother. Working on understanding and accepting her role in me hiding my authentic and true self has been a work in progress to say the least. As a child, I initially and intuitively trusted that my mother would be there to nurture and defend me. I did not have the words or the emotional ability to express that this abuse was wrong. It was not until I was an adult and made the decision to find myself that I was able to begin to interpret and understand her perspective. I was initially confused, and then deeply hurt as I started the process of unblocking and working through all aspects this chaos. I did not understand why she would turn her back on me. This piece of the puzzle is the most difficult to solve because, as any victim of abuse will tell you, the why is much more difficult to gain clarity about than the actual act. At some point, I just stopped trying to understand these parts, and decided to love and protect myself; I knew I could count on me, and I had to be enough so I could continue existing in this world.

After much therapy, coaching, and an abundance of self-love, self-care and the support of family and friends, I confronted and forgave my father. I also chose to forgive my mother for her role in allowing me to suffer while not protecting me from this horrible path I navigated. I worked through my loss of identity when I became the primary caregiver to my husband, and then struggled through the grief of his ultimate death. I did all of this for, what seemed like, endless years while focusing on and providing love and support to my children. As key motivators, they are the reason I am still standing after moving through all the hills and valleys of my feelings of "Who am I"; my children are the reason I have survived my adversities and achieved my eventual self-worth and personal growth. It was important for me to teach them that I could choose to take traumatic experiences in my life and use them to transition into an empowered, positive, strong and loving woman who was not willing to remain stuck in pain, loss and grief.

There were so many moments along the way when I thought I had figured myself out. Every now and again, I discovered little bits of awareness, and often felt that I reached that place of ultimate peace within the mystery of my life. But then, sometime later, I would discover the reality that there were more pieces yet to be solved. I felt fulfilled and frustrated at the same time, a combination of feelings of success mixed with feelings of defeat. I got used to these tiny victories mixed with setbacks and discovered that this was the process I needed to move through. I had to repeatedly break and repair. There was a continuous deep feeling that more needed to be uncovered before I would have the clarity I so desperately sought. I was determined to do the work but, I discovered that there were so many sides to my story, and I didn't have the capacity to investigate them all at once; I needed to break it all down and tackle one part at a time. Patience was truly a virtue as I focused intently to make sense of something that seemed so senseless. I used to think that if I could just uncover one part of it, all the rest would fall into place. What I learned is that it's just not that easy and there was no set way to get to where I wanted to go. I discovered that what happened to me was a blessing in disguise as it moved me to look at my past from the woman I am today. I am grateful for my current sense of self and my ability to love her. I am living life while questioning and pushing through fear and uncertainty, all while learning more about myself every day. If I never questioned or listened to my inner voice, I would always be stuck where I was, that little girl, the victim of abuse.

So, on a misty summer morning so long ago, I sat looking out onto a lake feeling lost and alone, and searching for the answer to the question that so many of us long for, "Who am I?" It was a terrifying place to be. From one moment to the next, I made a commitment to myself to find clarity about this mystery. It was the beginning of a long and difficult journey of self-discovery. I needed to find, know and then choose to love the woman I had become. I learned that for me to get from There to Here, I needed to find the courage to give my past a voice and speak my truth instead of hiding behind feelings of unworthiness, invisibility, ugliness and the expectation of perfection. I gave myself permission to find out who Donna had become as a result of her past experiences. Once discovered, I knew I would be able to accept this unique person, and then honor and love her unconditionally.

As I reflect, there were positive pieces within the negative ones but, at the time and through my healing, they were not in the forefront of my mind. The ones that had the most impact on me were the ones that had silenced my soul and inner voice. My emotional being struggled to survive; I felt broken. As a young girl, my father took my innocence from me by using my love for him as a tool to fulfill his sexual needs. The loss of the child within me came from his violation of me and what he asked me to do to please him. However, my innocence was compromised further because I was told to never share our secret. This immediately changed all I believed in. Before this happened, I was an innocent, joyful and curious little girl. My little girl's interpretation understood that I was asked to keep a secret but, I did not fully understand the impact of this secret until, as an adult, I started to unravel my story. Little Donna did not want people to know her secret, and I became distant, emotionally blocked and always striving to be a "good girl".

That girl believed that giving and receiving love meant doing what she was asked, keeping secrets, not drawing attention to herself, and that all of this equated to being that good little girl. My intuition told me that I should tell someone what was happening to me but, my sense of obligation to my father told me to do as he asked; he was my father, I loved him, and I must do as I was told. And I did.

"To keep this secret and continue to please my father, I had to find a way to mentally, emotionally and physically survive the fondling and sloppy kisses I remember enduring."

I remember pretending I was asleep when I heard his footsteps coming across the hall towards my bedroom. Since then, I have stored and locked away most of the horrible memories beyond the footsteps deep within a safe place inside of me. I subconsciously chose to protect myself, and that resulted in me blocking my memory from most of what happened. This all began around the age of 7, and this pattern of choosing not to remember created a sexual self that was void of human connection. I became disconnected from my emotional self, and I later became a sexual being void of feeling. I only understood sex as a physical act void of intimacy yet, still an obligation of what I understood love to be. Socially, I lost my voice and inhibited the ability to express myself. My choice of survival was to be a shy teenager, and low self-esteem became my defense by choosing to be invisible. It worked for me at the time as I could hide within the invisibility I created. The trade-off was that I felt ugly and unworthy of being seen or heard, and as a result, I became a target to be teased because I showed up as insecure and the boys found pleasure in bullying me and my twin sister. They gained power over me because I was afraid of them and what they thought of me, a pattern I developed under the control of my father.

At the age of 18, I had sex with a boy I barely knew. I remember my dad looking at me as I left on the date, and he told me to have a good time. My interpretation was that he meant it was ok to have sex with him. Looking back as a woman who has worked through the past, it seems so ridiculous but, as a teenager who had been abused by her father, that is what I understood and heard. I met my husband when I was 19. He was kind, caring, mature, and my knight in shining armor. I always dreamed of being a wife and mother, and I knew he would take care of me in a way that my father never had. In 1980, I married at the age of 21, and although my father's abuse ended when I was around 12 years old, I wanted to get out of the house and away from the man who continued to control me. I was married for 24 years, and I focused on being the best wife and mother I always dreamt of being; my husband made all the decisions and I cared for the family. Looking back, I now realize this became a role and I was not in touch with my femininity at all. Even though I loved my husband with all my heart, I never felt like a pretty or sensual woman because my past abuse programmed me to be numb to these feelings. Sex was still just a physical act, void of emotion and something that needed to get done to please the other person.

My husband was diagnosed with ALS in September of 1998. After some time, he could not speak, and he became totally paralyzed. I remember a moment when I found myself realizing that the caregiver burnout I was experiencing was not the only adversity that required healing. It came to light in a moment of intimacy between the two of us as I looked at him and saw his pleading eyes. I was stopped cold and broke down because I had seen those eyes many years before as a child. In that split second, I realized that my journey to heal and find myself encompassed more than just the recovery from years of caregiving, in that split second my childhood abuse rose to the surface, and a new layer of my past was revealed and screaming to be acknowledged. It was then that I made a promise to find Donna.

After 6 years of battling this debilitating disease, he passed away in November of 2004. When he died, nothing had been unsaid. We were married for 24 years and we fulfilled our vow of "till death do us part". I have two wonderful children who inherited beautiful traits from their dad. My love and memories of our family together will always be carried within my heart. Howevert, this was a very difficult time for me. I was trying to find myself, provide for my family and support my children emotionally and financially; they were 12 and 19 at the time. When I think back, I wonder how I did it. I know it was one day at a time and with the support of friends and family who provided me with love and hugs, encouraging words, and their time and energy. The commitment to my practice of journaling and meditation also provided me with the courage to step out of my fear and really looking at myself even if I didn't know the person staring back at me. Journaling was truly the most powerful tool and gift I gave myself as it provided my inner voice a place to be heard through the written word.

It was after mourning my husband that I realized I had lost myself through both the process of caring for him and my revelation that I was a victim of childhood abuse. I was unsure about who I was, and I decided to find clarity about who this person had become, including bits of old Donna mixed with the new. After years of absorbing wisdom in self-help books, taking care of my body by exercising, and mindfully journaling and meditating, I began to feel confident about emerging as the woman I was always meant to be. I had lost all of me so very long ago, and I knew who I was becoming was my authentic and true self because it felt comfortable and exciting. I created a clean slate and pushed through the fear of expressing myself. I was ready to show up as someone who was worthy to have an opinion and a unique way of being and share it all with my newfound voice. For so long, I went through life without the courage or the ability to speak my truth, and I could now express myself and believed I had something to say and that someone might just listen. I no longer needed to hide, and I could stand tall and confident in my truth, my story, and my life from a place of positive thoughts and my new, real way of being.

Looking back, my journey through the grief of my husband's death was easier than the journey of my childhood abuse, and it was time for me to share the latter with someone. But, beyond just telling anyone, I knew I had to speak my truth to my parents; I could not pretend my abuse didn't happen any longer. Dealing with the abuse as a child was painful and difficult. I had to go back to the little girl and experience the fear and the few memories that were breaking through. My daily journaling and meditation helped deal with the emotions and gave a voice to those thoughts and feelings.

Once I started this journey of self-discovery, I realized that I couldn't shut the door and ignore what was right in front of me. If I did that, I would have remained stuck in the past and not loved myself enough to let go of what was held locked up deep within my soul. I sought therapy and experienced anger and rivers of tears. I couldn't understand why this was happening to me. It didn't seem fair that in addition to me caring for my husband and supporting my children through their father's illness, I was now dealt the burden of managing my past.

The therapy provided me with the strength and courage to take the next step in healing by writing a letter to and facing my father, my abuser. I decided to take my life back. I have a voice. I will be heard, I matter.

"I remember the day I made the phone call to my parents. The night before I could not sleep as I felt like I was going to ruin everyone's life the next day."

I knew that my phone call would impact my entire family and life would never be the same. Mustering up the courage to experience this unveiling was one of the most difficult things I have ever done. It didn't compare to preparing for my husband's death. I could make sense of his leaving this world as he had a disease that no one survives but, confronting the two people who betrayed me was a completely different circumstance, and I was not sure what the outcome would be. All I knew was that I had no choice at this point in my life, I made a commitment to being Donna.

I was terrified but, I found the courage and called my mother. My hands and body shook as I dialed the phone. My mother answered, and I cried as I told her the secret. I could hear her turn to my dad, and he denied it. I met with the two people who I believed should have been my protectors, but instead one had sexually abused me and the other did not have the strength to stop it. I sat in front of them and read my letter as my hands shook with fear; I could barely read my writing through the tears and emotion. The words were spilled from my heart to express what happened and why I needed to expose the secret to heal myself and how it had impacted me. My parents sat in silence and listened to me. When I was done reading, my mother denied the abuse ever happened but, my father admitted that he did it. He said he was sorry and blamed my mother. She sat silent for a moment and then said, "Don't tell your brothers." Another secret was made as I did not have the strength to tell my brothers at that time; that secret would be unveiled years later. My sisters already knew because they too were abused by my father.

It was the most difficult conversation I ever had but, it was a necessary one for me to take my power back, and one that changed everyone in my family from that day forward. I cannot say it made our lives easier or better but, the elephant stood up and walked out of the room. The truth was acknowledged, and we were all freed from the lies and deception; we were given the choice to move forward knowing that the past was uncovered and there may even be a chance of forgiveness. I felt I did the right thing for my sisters as I gave them the chance to embrace freedom from the sexual abuse and the opportunity to delve into their own personal work and move towards healing their past. Because I spoke my truth, I managed to stop the cycle of abuse for future generations by standing up and saying, "NO MORE!"

Then the trade-off came of knowing I just shattered my parents' lives. I had to work through the guilt of exposing the family secret to heal myself. This, of course, impacted my parents' relationship because they both had to live with the truth being told. I knew I would always be the daughter who came forward and exposed the dark family secret. I continued to journal and work through my emotions. I listened to what came up, and I focused on discovering my purpose in life. I discovered that finding people and activities that touched me in some way helped me to heal one day at a time.

Those two years of difficult work brought me to the uncomfortable place of facing my father with a voice and ability to express myself. He took my innocence so long ago, and I courageously took the journey I never thought I would ever be able to travel. Although, I always knew that my past affected my life and my choices, one of my greatest epiphanies is the extent to which my decisions were influenced by my past abuse and how it affected my relationships with my father and mother. Even more impactful is how these choices influenced my destiny and where I ultimately landed. I am so grateful for the inner voice within me that continues to move beyond fear to experience life and to find lessons in all my experiences.

My past became a part of me, my choices and my entire way of being. Even to this day, I need to be mindful about and manage what bubbles up within an instant, a memory, a word, a situation or a certain person and how they may speak or what they say can trigger U-turns and steps back from the growth I achieved. But, I know that this is all part of my path of self-discovery and what I am intended to experience and learn. I know in order for me to grow, I must value acceptance and only then can I choose to move forward.

However, understanding the belief of acceptance was not enough as I needed to take it a step further and practice and commit to what I said I valued. I needed to be provided with the opportunity to embrace acceptance so that I could experience it with grace and gratitude. This turning point presented itself when my father became ill and was admitted into the hospital in 2015. The universe provided me with time alone with him. I sat in his room beside him as he sat by the window, and he began to cry. He said he was sorry and asked if I hated him. I knelt down by him with my hand in his, and I said, "No, Dad I don't hate you. I forgive you and I love you." The words just flowed out of me without any thought or effort so, I knew I meant what I was sharing with him, the man who gave me life along with so much pain. It was in this moment I realized that for me to continue living my life with any kind of peace, I had to provide forgiveness to my father who had abused me at such a young age. My days of choosing to show up as a victim were over; I would now choose to be a survivor, able to forgive and live in gratitude for the lessons I was given. I would do whatever I had to do to show up in this world as the best version of myself. It was on this day that I chose to give myself the gift of freedom by releasing my past, along with all that I had suffered, while also giving my father the gift of unconditional forgiveness and love.

With this newfound freedom of acceptance, I forged ahead with the next step in my process of healing. I knew I had to work through my anger and feelings of abandonment created by my mother's choice to cast a blind eye on her husband's abusive behavior towards her daughter. I had to provide her with the same forgiveness I gave my father, even if I could not understand why she did not protect me from my father's abuse.

"Eventually, I understood that my mother did not have the capacity to stand up for herself or for her children as she too was abused as a young girl and suffered the anguish of living with her own victimization."

Emotional and behavioral patterns are difficult to shift, especially for that generation. Once I revealed my abuse, and before my mother passed away, I tried to have a meaningful relationship with her but, in her eyes, I was not the one who began a path of familial healing but instead, the one who created more damage and pain; she believed I should have let it be. I now know she lived with great shame, and for that I have compassion for her. I know she would not admit this but, she believed she needed to block what she felt she could not face. I can only imagine the guilt she must have been tormented with until the day she died. I know she loved me deeply but, did not have the capacity to express it openly.

After all my work moving through the abuse and my ultimate healing, it may be difficult to understand I loved both of my parents dearly. They provided me with lessons that contributed to pieces of my best self. They taught me positive learnings and values that serve me to this day. During years of healing, I developed personal empowerment by setting boundaries with each of them around behavior I considered unacceptable. I let them know that I chose to live from a place of positivity and I could not be a part of their lives if they chose to be angry and negative. This allowed me to create the space I needed to heal and move forward living a life of joy, happiness and truth. I took my life back, and I love the woman I have grown into, every single piece of me, including what was created from the abuse and abandonment. The courage I found to face my parents was developed by what they did to me. Because of their choices, I became determined to work through the anger, hurt and fear and find a place of peace and love. Without paying attention to my inner voice nudging me, I would never have discovered who I am from the depth of my soul; I may very well still be wondering, "Who is Donna?"

My parents died in 2015 within four months of each other. It was then that I realized they had lived in complete co-dependence of one another. My mother chose my father over me during my childhood, and then again at the end of his life by following him in death. She could not face life without him. It is with gratitude that I acknowledge they are now at peace together. I believe their deaths provided me with the space I needed to heal myself further. As sad as it may sound, in leaving this earth, they provided me with the opportunity to focus on extensive healing without the guilt and knowledge that the more I moved forward, the more I left them behind. With their passing, came the blessing of freedom to no longer feel invisible and unworthy but instead, to love and accept all of who I am. I longed for this freedom of space, time and energy to make sense of my journey and the path that destiny has in store for me, to understand where I came from, my past, and where I was heading, my future. It was critical for me to find clarity and forgiveness about which pieces of my past I wanted to keep as part of who I am and which pieces I would choose to let go of, those that didn't serve me anymore. This clarity and awareness took me to another piece of the puzzle of rebuilding my life and truly knowing me on a deep and personal level.

"One might think this story concludes with the uncovering of the gifts of acceptance and gratitude I received. However, I found that with each piece of healing, yet another opportunity of growth presented itself."

Even though my husband and I lived together as a couple, over time, we had long lost any intimate connection we once had due to the progression of his disease. With the diagnosis of his terminal illness, my life quickly shifted from the fairy tale story I dreamed of as wife and mother to his caretaker and lifeline. Simultaneously, I worked full-time, cared for my children, and eventually provided an ALS support group in my home. My life's focus was providing support to him and others, becoming physically active and continuing to work on myself.

It was three years after my husband's passing when I realized I was ready to move on and begin dating as my newfound Donna. I was ready to give and receive within a new relationship and share myself with someone else. I felt excited, positive and confident, and I thought I was emotionally ready to take this step into the unknown. Little did I know there would be another set of obstacles waiting for me and they would be deeply connected to the abuse I thought I had overcome. Once again, I would be getting back on that wheel of taking great steps forwards and then a few backwards to discover even more about myself; the scars re-surfaced.

It became obvious that I did not fully acknowledge the depth of the subconscious patterns I had been carrying and showed up throughout my life. It was when I yearned for the touch of a man again that I was awakened to the work that still needed to be done. I was called to connect with my sexual being and the woman within me. It took some time for me to discover that I could combine the two while creating a physical and emotional sexual experience, one that tapped into my primal side as well as the tender and loving feminine side that did not exist within my marriage. I have not had many sexual experiences since my husband's death, and I think of these men as my teachers and these experiences as lessons I needed to learn. I am grateful for each as they taught me many things. In my 50's, they took me through the sexual process and exploration I was denied as a teenager, as well as, through great growth through this new journey.

I courageously entered the dating world which I was never a part of; it was all new to me having met my husband at 19, being married at 21 and finding myself a widow at 45. I had clarity about the discomfort and the insecurity my abuse created surrounding men, but I jumped into dating with hope and great expectations of finding a new kind of love. I met a kind, compassionate man who I connected with immediately, and we could talk for hours. I was not quite prepared for the, almost immediate, intensity of the physical aspect of our relationship. I had not been touched in an intimate way for years, and when I was, it was like a lightning surge of energy from one body to another. I was like a freight train in this first encounter as a single woman. I found myself moving towards old sexual patterns of moving too fast, and this left him feeling overwhelmed. When he brought this to my attention, I felt hurt, humiliated and embarrassed and in need of more self-reflection. I voiced my accountability and acknowledged my part in moving too fast and understanding his feelings of needing to slow down.

Our relationship moved to pure friendship and remained there for a very long time. He became my sounding board and someone I could talk to easily. I had fallen in love with the fantasy of a relationship with him. Feelings of unworthiness came up, and I made the decision to move on.

I soon recognized that I needed to take time to understand that I was picking people emotionally unavailable because I had also been emotionally blocked for so long that I was unable to fully experience a healthy relationship. This was a very difficult lesson to learn because I had to acknowledge and accept the work that still needed to be done on my quest to experiencing a relationship with another man. With every lesson comes more self-awareness and the epiphanies of life. I realized I had to love all of me before anyone else could love me. I found clarity that the man I choose to love will love all pieces of me as I love and accept myself. My purpose within a relationship is not to rescue or heal the person I am with. I can be in a wonderful relationship with a man who is confident with himself as I am with myself, and as a result, experience a healthy relationship. With this newfound awareness, I could look back on my life clearly and see my awakening as the woman I truly am with all the good, bad and even the ugly.

I did not date again for several years. I had much work to do on my emotional well-being, and I realized that the subconscious habits and stories I learned from an early age could still be released and replaced with new patterns and positive beliefs. It was time to really make sense of my abuse and focus on getting to know myself before I considered another relationship with a man. I was not in a place that I could share all of me because I had not been introduced to the entirety of Donna yet.

I turned back to the meditation and journaling I practiced for years prior. I worked through my emotions to reveal the answers and provide the lessons I needed to move forward. The self-awareness fell upon me like a ton of bricks. I was the common denominator in my failed attempts at dating and moving on. It was a reminder that the abuse I endured created a response to love that had become second nature to me. Subconsciously, a message was being sent to me that became an expectation when I was with a man. There was a voice in my head telling me I was not worthy of anything other than being a physical vessel to be used for sex, and I agreed with it by showing up as that story dictated. The story was developed by a fear of being abandoned by the people I love. My father abandoned me when I was too old to meet his physical needs, my mother turned her back on me when she chose not to protect me from his abuse and my husband left me with his tragic death.

I awoke to the fact that if I wanted a relationship with a man that included love, compassion, self-worth and respect, I needed to be accountable for the part I played in not receiving these beautiful characteristics of love I so deeply valued. I also recognized that the man I choose to be with needed to value the same type of love I was craving. As I became intimately aware of my soulful self, I began to get to know my physical, sensual and sexual self. This allowed me to be more confident and aware of my true feelings and sensations within my body which, in turn, created an empowerment I have never experienced before. The confidence of clarity created excitement knowing I can be truly whole again and not be held back by my past.

Through this journey, I discovered the most difficult part of healing and moving forward is being honest with myself and owning the parts of me I don't find very complimentary. I am aware of my imperfections, and I accept them as I cannot be perfect. I also learned to pay attention to my inner nudges as they are always right. I am committed to understanding my values and making daily choices in line with what I believe in. In writing this story, I realize I had to come to this place in my life to really see and understand all of me. I have been emotionally unavailable for so long that it makes sense I would pick men equally emotionally detached as they mirror that part of me.

I am still healing and know that life is a journey with many twists and turns. I choose to live all of life's moments, and I believe that every day is a gift. I refuse to take any moment for granted as I live life from a place of love, rather than fear. I am excited and blessed to have taken the time to listen to my inner voice and to let my intuition guide me. I know I will never have life completely figured out but, I also know I have choices to make every day to make my life rich and full. It is the way in which I choose to respond to the challenges and the accomplishments that will impact me and the people in my life. I have a desire to make a difference, and maybe that difference will be made by simply being myself. I am enough, and I love the woman I have become.

I DISCOVERED THE FEELING OF CALM

HOW DONNA INSPIRES CALM

Donna has lived in Kingston, Ontario her entire life. This year, she is retiring from a 36-year career as an Administrative Assistant in a local hospital. She is a mother of two wonderful children who are moving on with their own lives and paths. Never taking mobility for granted, Donna keeps fit and challenges her body with cycling, swimming, strength training and running.

Donna enjoys connecting with family and friends, and her goal in life has always been to make a difference in people's lives by being herself and sharing what she can to support others coping with loneliness.

Her past volunteer experience includes supporting families for the ALS Society of Ontario, the ALS Rehab Clinic and her local Hospice Bereavement Support Group. Donna also facilitated an ALS support group in her home.

Donna has moved through the stages of grief and self-discovery over the past 15 years to become the woman she is today. She hopes that sharing her story will give others hope and inspiration to move forward to discover what life has to offer beyond what feels painful and unfair.

Donna found that, even though happiness often seemed so far away, with determination and courage, everything fell into place when the time was right. It was then when she arrived at a place of peace, joy and contentment.

She learned that life is always moving and presenting new experiences and adventures that allow her to discover more about herself. She focuses on living in the present, facing her fears and enjoying the highs while moving through the lows with the gentleness of calm and understanding.

You can discover more about Donna by connecting with her at donna_17@live.ca

INTRODUCING
TANA HEMINSLEY

The day I met Tana Heminsley in the spring of 2011, I knew my life was about to change for the better; I could feel it. There was an aura about her that said, "Welcome, you are home". I left her presence that day feeling like everything was going to be alright .

I evolved more than I ever thought I was capable of as a result of meeting Tana; I consider her my mentor and very good friend. But, more impactful for me is that she showed me, just by her way of being, what it means to truly lead with integrity, to place ego on the shelf and to delve deep into self-discovery, and, amidst all the adversity and the chaos of the unknown in this universe, to use self-love and love for others to evolve as a better person. She is the epitome of compassion.

Tana's way of showing up in the world models what authenticity looks and feels like. No matter who you are or what you are going through, Tana supports humankind in finding clarity about where you want to be, what you want to do and who you are within it all. And she does all of this with, what feels like, incredible grace and ease.

You are about to experience Tana's Story[5] of
From There to Here **and how she discovered the feeling of**
Inner Peace

Diane Bayer

---

[5]This Chapter is an excerpt from the soon to be published 2nd edition of "Awaken Your Authentic Leadership –Lead from Inner Clarity and Purpose," Tana Heminsley

From There to Here;

Inner Peace

By Tana Heminsley

Inner Peace

™

Tana's Story

I love how Diana describes life as a road trip with many detours along the way. My road trip includes my life experiences and career, along with my inner awareness of thoughts and emotions that made me who I am today. My life has been amazing, and at the same time, I experienced levels of inner turmoil beyond the normal maturation and growth process. I ignored, uncovered and moved through that inner turmoil towards inner peace.

The inner work I committed to was crucial as it made possible the healing essential to my wellness of mind, body and spirit. The result of this work provided me with the ability to cultivate my potential, create psychological safety, along with the richness of the quality of life I aspired to.

For more than 30 years while in business, I studied how individuals overcame childhood trauma to go on to become successful organizational leaders. I extensively researched the inner journey of leaders and how it relates to long-term behavioral change and the recovery of unhealed issues. At first, I didn't realize this was meant to support me on my road trip; I thought it was about others.

Respecting confidentiality is paramount to me. I would, therefore, like to thank my family and friends as they have, and still do, provide essential support that makes my continual road trip possible. I apologize because I am, of course, Canadian and that's what we do, for choosing not to share the support I received from them along the way in order to respect confidentiality.

Digging the Hole

I was born in Revelstoke, British Columbia, Canada in 1962. For the first 28 years of my existence, I lived on autopilot as I was unaware of the possibility of inner work and I let life happen to me. I dug a hole of self-destruction, and relished being in it. In elementary school, I was the good girl and the smart one. I had a wonderful family and I have fond memories of family trips, staying with aunts, uncles and cousins, flying with my dad, gathering with my large extensive family at my grandmother and grandfather's home, learning piano and guitar, and growing up with my brothers.

On the other hand, I remember in grade three, playing dumb at math to get attention from the teacher. And so, something changed, and things began to shift.

I became rebellious in high school and had many boyfriends. I picked a few doozies. I remember one who drove by the clothing store where I worked; he had been drinking. He jumped off the back of a pick-up truck in front of the store, came inside and threw a diamond "promise ring" down on the counter. He then turned around and got back on the truck. He was the same one who later organized a "house wrecking" party and orchestrated the actual ruining of the interior of a beautiful old home. I remember being shocked and thinking "This isn't right." Yet, I did nothing because I wanted to fit in. I partied hard along with him and my friends, and I tested my parents' and my bosses' limits.

I had nightmares. They were mostly about an intense fear of someone coming to get me in the darkness. I had a recurring dream where I was chased by a grizzly bear in the night and, when it got close, I jumped up and flew over the trees. There was a full moon and the peaceful feeling of flying kept me safe. It was years later that I discovered this was a form of dissociation from my body and my experience. I realize now that while I had a wonderful, normal upbringing, I didn't like myself. I received self-esteem from external sources at that time. I believed that if I had a boyfriend, I was ok and valuable. While in their presence, I felt a false sense of worth until it slowly dissipated along with them walking away.

"I could feel myself digging deeper into a hole, and I knew something was wrong with how I felt about myself, life and, in particular, the way my mind worked against me. I just didn't know how to change any of it. I yearned to lift myself out of the hole early on so, I decided to try out a few things to see which ones felt right for me."

One was a treatment centre where I worked with several counsellors and read an endless number of books including

Stephen Covey's Seven Habits of Highly Successful People. I remember giving the first copy away as I wasn't ready for it, and then a few years later, buying another one and devouring its contents. It remains one of my favourite resources. I listened to personal development tapes, talked to people who inspired me, and set personal goals for the first time in my life.

I worked on building my competency around public speaking because it terrified me!! I joined Toastmasters, and during one of the exercises to become comfortable standing up in front of a crowd of people, I was asked to, spontaneously, talk for 2 minutes about a random topic. I had to "describe a snowflake." I remember spending the longest, most uncomfortable two minutes of my life searching for something to say. I quit shortly afterwards. Then a year or so later, I re-joined and moved quickly through the ranks, from participant to member of the executive, and finally, local chapter President.

I learned that timing is everything and that I needed to be patient and completely ready for each stage of my progression order for it to be effective.

Sitting in the Hole

I had amazing adventures in my early life that included working in Corporate Communications on the Rogers Pass Tunnel Project for CP Rail when I was only 21. I had an incredible boss who gave me autonomy, as well as, coaching focused on me being my best. Part of my position was providing project tours to guests. They included CBC and Anne Medina who covered the $600M project, a group of local Boy Scouts who wanted to plant trees alongside the railway line and an Ambassador from France who was checking out tunnel ventilation systems for possible use in the Chunnel between France and England.

I got to work with a photographer and write articles for CP Rail's national newsletter. One time, we had to take a small mining train into a tunnel for 6 kilometers and climb through an 18-inch motor hole of a tunnel boring machine in order to write an article about how it worked.

In 1986 at the age of 24, I got married for the first time. I quit university 2 weeks into the 4th year of my undergrad degree in order to move in with my husband in Revelstoke. Even though I felt strong within my career, I completely lost my sense of self during this marriage; I didn't realize this until I got divorced in 1988. We were young, drank too much, and lacked maturity within our relationship. This marriage provided me with an initial awakening that intimacy was difficult for me. I actually dreaded it when I was aware, sober and present. When I was drunk or high, it was great. I remember expressing the uncomfortable level of anxiety I experienced when thinking about physical intimacy to one of my counsellors; I described it as "finger nails being scraped down a chalkboard."

As I neared my divorce, my lifestyle became even more unhealthy as I searched for an external source of internal peace and worthiness. I partied way too much. Every Friday night I drank double martinis with my colleagues to wash away my week.

"I went to a Saturday session with a counsellor who suggested that I might be an alcoholic and that I needed to go to a treatment centre right away. At the time, I remember thinking that I must be an alcoholic if she believed I was."

I found irony in the fact that I would be spending 28 days in a treatment centre in Napa Valley, the wine capital of USA. It sounded like a spa-holiday to me!

I thought I had nothing to lose and it would give me some much-needed space from my ex-husband in order to gain perspective about what was happening and where I was headed. On that Sunday, the day after my session with her, I agreed to go into treatment; I was on a plane Monday morning. It was one of the best and most difficult things I ever did for myself. It provided me with the start to a life of personal development, along with the first glimpses of the steps I needed to dig myself out of the hole.

As the security guard picked me up at the San Francisco airport and we drove to Napa and up "Sanatorium Road", I remember feeling terrified and wondering what I had got myself into. For 28 days, I ate healthy vegetarian food, attended counselling sessions, learned about family dynamics and the role I took on as the oldest child. I also learned the importance of being mature enough to actually feel the discomfort of uncomfortable experiences, how to be vulnerable and cry while letting my guard down.

I attended AA meetings and practiced saying "Hi, I'm Tana and I'm an alcoholic." After three weeks, the counsellor at the centre asked me why I was there. I told him that I thought I was an alcoholic. He paused and said we don't think you are. I said then I must be in denial. He told me that if I was in denial, I wouldn't say I was in denial. He agreed to allow me to finish the program if I wanted to, but that he didn't see alcoholism as an issue for me. He believed that I was close to crossing the line from social to problem drinking, and that I needed to watch my step and be more aware of this for the future. I decided to stay through the final week of the program and graduation. While there, I continued to work-out twice a day. I absorbed all kinds of personal-development information and practices focused on learning how to feel emotions and deal with stress effectively. I also discovered what Alcoholics Anonymous and other 12-step recovery programs were all about and the value they provide.

Before leaving, I was required to set up an aftercare program. Part of this included setting up counselling for a year after I returned home. This counselling supported me in working through the next phase of self-discovery as I began sorting through the unhelpful aspects of my personality and how it impacted me and others. I realized that on the outside I had this incredible life, while on the inside, I was living mostly in survival mode. I made destructive choices because I didn't like myself, rather than choosing to reach for my potential.

I had no idea what my potential was. I just knew that my way of living had stopped working for me.

By 1989, at the age of 27, and after returning from the treatment centre, I divorced and started my next incredible adventure. My parents' belief in me always astounded me. They agreed to co-sign a loan so, I could start my own clothing store. I never ran a business before so, I had a lot to learn. The store was called "Tana Lee". I loved the business, building relationships and spending time with clients. My mom and friends worked there with me, and we had fashion shows in the downtown plaza and the best window displays in town. I handpicked clothing for clients at the buy shows and, learned how to make successful business decisions while reaping the rewards.

I remember thinking that going to buy shows and having all the clothes I wanted would make me happy. And yet, I found I was still unsettled. Recently divorced, not having completed my university education, and unhappy in my personal relationships, I yearned for an extraordinary life. I just didn't know what that looked like or how to achieve it. I had no sense of who I was or what my value as a person was. It wasn't until much later that I realized that my value arises simply because I am a human being, living on this earth.

I remember the day, a man I was going out with, arrived at the store and told me I had hurt him deeply. He told me I was self-centred and immature within my relationships. In that moment, I remember thinking that things had to change, and I couldn't keep living like this, treating others unkindly and living with so much dysfunction. In that moment, I woke up, for real this time, and actually saw myself in the hole of my own making. Even with this huge awakening, I still didn't know how deep the hole was. So, I continued on my journey, digging away, hopeful I would eventually find my way out of it.

I received one of the best pieces of advice from a counsellor who supported me in the year after the treatment centre. "It was my responsibility to give myself the life I wanted and to treat myself as I expected others to treat me, with respect and kindness, and then others would treat me the same way". Realizing later that this translated into my creating an extraordinary life, whether I was in a relationship or not, provided me with reflection and clarification about what my values were. Once I understood what was deeply important to me, I set some goals, and had more of an idea about where I was headed. Suddenly, opportunities seemed to appear.

Two women who wanted to buy my clothing store approached me, and I jumped at the opportunity to sell. I then took a trip to Vancouver and got a job in the fashion retail industry at Fairweather. I worked hard as the assistant manager and was promoted to manager at their flagship downtown store which produced $3M in annual sales, had a 10,000-unit inventory and 35 employees on the team; quite a leap from my little store in Revelstoke.

Then, I felt unsettled once again.

I discovered that fashion and store operations weren't where I was meant to be. The numbers game was draining me; 10,000 units in, 10,000 units out, hourly targets and the continual folding of thousands of sweaters. I realized that my life had become a cycle of coaching staff, making targets and folding sweaters in an underground mall, and I knew I wanted something different. My team was my saving grace. I am so grateful for all I learned from my relationships with them, especially how to support others through their personal and professional growth, how to be successful while being able to be myself with them, and to take care of myself without being taking advantage of by my peers or my staff. I learned all of these wonderful things and more. But at the same time, I was unhappy, and I had a bad attitude.

On the other hand, I was so fortunate to be given an incredible boss. She sat me down and said, "We think you have a future here, but you're going to have to change a few things." What an awakening. I hated hearing it and yet, I needed to hear it. I feel blessed that she didn't fire me on the spot because she saw my potential and gave me the opportunity to do the right thing for me and the company. It was a turning point as I realized that I could choose a positive attitude or a negative one. It was my choice to stay or leave.

So, choose I did! I stayed, and I scraped up every extra cent I had and invested in an executive development program to help me determine what I loved. It encompassed mentoring, reviewing job descriptions, engaging in informational interviews, and completing psychometric assessments to help determine what I was passionate about. Once again, I was lost and didn't know where I was headed, but I knew that I needed to do this personal work in order to figure it all out.

And so, the climbing out of the hole extended to much, much more than just the psychological aspects of recovery. I made a bucket list of challenges I believed I needed to conquer to achieve the happiness and purpose I was seeking. Twelve years after quitting university in 4th year to get married, I determined that it was time for me to go back to complete my undergraduate degree. In order to be considered for the post-graduate program, I needed to improve my marks very quickly. I needed to be accepted into a masters in business administration (MBA) program, and I needed to determine how I would finance it at a price of about $22K for 2 years. This was an enormous obstacle for me at the time as I was working full time and living on a retail store manager's annual salary of $45K. I wasn't sure when I would even find the time to go to school and study, and I also needed to pass the pre-requisite GMAT test and get accepted into the program. I did it all.

I decided to shift my mindset, and with great determination, I overcame each obstacle. With the help of a tutor, I finally passed the GMAT test on the third try after failing it two times in a row. Third time really is a charm!! I was accepted into and began the Simon Fraser University Executive MBA Program, all while managing to finance it by working at Fairweather.

There were many character-building moments as I struggled to achieve this life-changing goal. I remember, a few months into the program, walking out of a calculus refresher course, which was ironic because I had never taken the original course in the first place. I went into the bathroom, sat on the floor in the stall and cried. My mind was racing, "How did I think I could do this?" "What was I doing here?" Honestly, I had no idea just how strong my inner critical voice was at that time, or even that I had one. And then, I told myself to just go back into the hall, keep taking notes, go to all the group tutorials, talk to the other students, and, at some point, the light will go on, and I would, eventually, understand it. And I did.

I finished my EMBA, gave notice at Fairweather, and more than doubled my salary as soon as I walked out of the mall for the last time. The EMBA provided me with new concepts to draw upon in my business and leadership "tool box". I had a new level of confidence and a new community of friends and colleagues.

Lifting Myself Out of the Hole

I realize now that lifting myself out of the hole started in part, earlier in life and without awareness. At some point it became intentional and my driving force.

As part of the completion of my undergrad degree in Criminology, I deepened my research on violence against women and adults who had experienced childhood trauma. As a result of delving into this journey, I experienced several awakenings. The biggest one occurred when I was attending a psychology course as part of my undergrad degree in Vancouver while, simultaneously, managing the Fairweather store. I remember sitting in a cavernous lecture hall, along with hundreds of others, listening to a lecture on violence against women. The professor spoke about adult children of child sexual trauma and the impact on them moving into adulthood. The symptoms include destructive behavior, several forms of addiction, nightmares, the inability to tolerate certain physiological sensations in the body, types of dissociation, lack of boundaries, dysfunctional relationships, and the list went on. I felt like the lecture was about me and that the researchers used my life in their studies; it was as if they had followed me around and read my diary. I was thirty-three years old, and suddenly the personal challenges made sense in a way I never understood.

In that moment, I felt the room close in on me. I experienced a vacuum-like feeling in my body; time seemed to stand still. My entire attention focused on me sitting in that hall. I became clear and incredibly present to that one moment. I instantly woke up to knowing how deep the hole I was living in was and how much I experienced every part of my life through the distorted lens it created.

I realized that something bad had happened to me when I was a child.

Another, even darker awakening occurred next. It became the darkest moment from which I would ever recover. A few months later, I had an acute realization that the one thing I ran from my entire life was not something or someone outside of me, but rather, something inside my body, something inside my mind; I discovered that it was me.

"The conscious knowing that I was unable to flee the shame, self-loathing, anger and self-destruction that had been plaguing me since I was a young girl, was almost too much. I knew that I needed to reach out."

I am grateful I received support from good friends who helped me move away from the metaphorical edge of the abyss of what the hole could have become. Pulling myself out of this pit of devastation became the most difficult part of my journey. Recovering from any trauma is no small thing, and it takes time and immense patience. I realize this now as I write my "From There to Here" at the beginning of my 55th year.

I'm 90 percent there. The old layers of awareness still show up once in a while to remind me of my constant companions, the nightmares occur much less frequently now, and the ghosts of feelings and emotions, uncomfortable body memories and the resulting feelings of shame and anger linger as a result of still-unknown traumatic experiences that happened so many years ago.

Time went on, and I was happy and enjoying a healthy relationship for the first time. I had a successful career as an executive, and I did enough personal work that the implications of the childhood trauma hurdles no longer ruled my life. I was able to move into the light of life's possibilities thanks to the 13 counsellors, therapists and coaches, personal development workshops, and the 28-day stint in the treatment centre. Each support person and program provided me with the courage to get in touch with the mother lode of anger and shame that was the result of the trauma I experienced as a child.

As I let go of the unhelpful aspects of my personality and shifted old unhelpful beliefs, doors opened that would, otherwise, never have been available to me.

One was an 8-year adventure with BC Hydro, a multi-billion-dollar hydro-electric utility company. I had the privilege of working in several positions at BC Hydro including project manager for a multi-year, company-wide strategy implementation project. This turned out to be one of my great accomplishments, as well as, one of my failures; I am thankful for these as I learned a lot and was immensely humbled. Later, I assisted the CEO from a strategic perspective, and ultimately participated as a member of the executive leadership team who oversaw the organization.

During that 8-year period, I left and returned to the company several times. At one point, I moved to Chicago and worked for a world-renowned consulting firm called the Balanced Scorecard Collaborative. They were located outside

Boston, and my clients spanned the US, including an energy company in New Orleans and a medical system in Duluth, Minnesota.

I managed to squeeze in seeing the Institute of Art in Chicago on the few weekends I was actually there, but my life mainly consisted of Monday morning cab rides to the airport and Thursday evenings heading home from a client site in another state. There were a lot of storms in the mid-west that year, and I remember flights diverting around tornados and lightening, as well as being stuck overnight in airports more than a few times, along with many other members of the consulting subculture. We lived tethered to our laptops and cell phones in our virtual, airport offices.

One day while waiting for a plane, I had an epiphany that I was satisfied with nothing and nothing could happen fast enough. I was constantly frustrated, and I drove myself harder and harder. The stress was beginning to show physically, and, at its worst, I had cold sores on a weekly basis. My immune system was in trouble. Success lost its meaning as I equated it to knowing that I was smart enough and capable enough to play in that big U.S. game. Having an EMBA and making big money was what I thought I was supposed to aspire to and achieve. I thought that if clients sought me out and wanted to work with me, and if others viewed me as smart, I must be a good person and be of value. I discovered that progress isn't linear. Here I was, back to the question of worth as a human being.

I knew there was something more.

Upon reflection, I was probably burned out at the beginning of my move to the U.S. After six months of heavy travel, including one week that entailed eight flights, I was definitely past the point of emotional and physical exhaustion. I began to question what it all meant. By cultural standards, I had the material success I was supposed to strive for. I was able to take more cabs, eat at better restaurants and take more holidays. I recognized that I went to the U.S. in large part to satisfy the unhelpful aspects of my ego. I remember having a conversation on the phone with my Mom and Dad and he said, "You know, you can get off that ladder you are climbing. Where are you climbing to anyway?" I thought a lot about that conversation, and I realized that my life was back in Canada and I needed to get off the ladder I was climbing to who knows where.

I also recognized that my life seemed happier when I was being choice-ful by creating it my way, and not waiting for someone or something to rescue me and make me feel better. So, I quit my job in the U.S. and moved back to Vancouver and BC Hydro.

Thank goodness, I did!

When I returned home, I met Chris. He is the man of my dreams, and we continue to have an extraordinary life together. We are two peas in a pod; we talk about everything, we travel, and spend time with our friends and family. Chris and I live in our dream home in downtown Vancouver with our cat, Buddy.

After leaving the U.S., my personal life was high on the happiness meter. However, the career question came up again while on the executive team at BC Hydro. How much harder did I want to work? How many more hours and groups did I have the capacity to take on? Did I really want to pursue a senior executive position? I moved beyond my capacity a second time and realized that I was letting my ego drive the bus again. I could feel that I was getting my self-esteem from my job instead of from just being me.

The wake-up call was loud and clear.

I was choosing to live beyond my capacity AGAIN, and

this time, and for several years after, it manifested physically as adrenal fatigue, hormonal imbalance and vertigo. The way I lived wasn't working for me anymore, and I knew something was still blocked. I sought support from my doctor, a naturopath and counsellor; it was time for another major life change. I sought counselling to understand and overcome old, unhelpful behaviours and attitudes that were continuing to limit me, and I read The Power of Intention by Dr. Wayne Dyer. I began to gain more clarity about my purpose and what I was intended for on this earth. As a result of the years of counselling and all this personal development work, I gained clarity about what I was meant to do with my life.

"One day while practicing yoga, the ability to actually articulate it became very clear; I wanted to be "a source for others to realize and live their lives to their full potential." I wanted to be a guide for others to be intentional about their personal journey."

Further clarity came soon after when I discovered I wanted to do this with leaders in the business world in order to support them on their personal-development journey. I knew I wanted to use the things I learned and my life experiences to help others. I felt an urgency to support them in starting their journey to authenticity as soon as possible in order to improve the quality of their lives forever.

This would be my way to support peace – through inner peace one person at a time - to alleviate pain and suffering in the world. These instantly became my new mantras.

I was so confident and clear about my new path that I gave notice and started to think about my next business. My old pattern was to get busy and write a plan, get into my head and sort out the business model. This time, I spent almost two years researching, trying out new things, and processing everything before I began planning. I wanted life to unfold to see my direction more clearly before I put it in writing. I began a year-long professional Integral Coaching program with New Ventures West in San Francisco. When I entered the classroom for the first time, it felt like I had come home. I discovered others who were on the same path, and I was blessed with a new community of support.

Through counselling and coaching, along with the nutritional and philosophical support of my doctor and naturopath, I learned to achieve balance again and how to integrate it into my life (more of the time, not yet all of the time). I learned to live with inner clarity about who I am as my Authentic or Best Self versus the unhelpful aspects of my personality, my ego. I learned how to live with self-compassion and joy more of the time, versus fear and anger.

I experienced a huge shift during an introduction to the Enneagram system when I learned that I was a Type Three or "Achiever". Although, this was not a big surprise, the real learning was the new awareness that I sought self-esteem from external sources, rather than from inner clarity. At my worst, I needed to be considered successful by what others expected of me and wear the badge of an executive to feel worthy. Failing to meet these requirements was too distressing to even contemplate. I suddenly woke up for the first time to the fact that I still lived my life in a way that wasn't honouring my Authentic Self or my full potential.

This realization introduced me to a strong foundation of practices that support me to live from what my heart wants and lead from authenticity more of the time. This is in contrast to living only as part of my potential, who I am when living from my old, automatic patterns or default way-of-being. While the strengths of my personality have helped me be very successful, the unhelpful aspects no longer serve me. My years of extensive inner development work supported me to remember who I am as my Authentic or Best self.

From these awakenings, Authentic Leadership Global, Inc. was born; one of my proudest accomplishments.

Leaving the Hole Behind

From that time on until present day, things significantly changed for me for the better. I have a wonderful family and incredible friends who I am able to call upon for support and who I'm able to be there for as well. Although, internally and once in a while, I find myself back at the edge of the hole looking down into it, the difference is that I am now able to see the hole of my past in front of me and choose not to jump into it. I can, consciously, live my life in service of others, and I have clarity and am aligned with who I am as my best and Authentic Self.

I, finally, like myself and enjoy more contentment and inner peace than I ever experienced before. The need for therapeutic tune-ups are much less frequent as I settled in my own skin and can see all of life as a gift and my experiences as keys to my foundation and strength. I now have the capacity and empathy to support others to discover whatever path their journey may take them on.

Even though I still find the active practice of balance a challenge at times, the possibilities for my life are now endless, and the pace is manageable. I experience more inner peace and self-confidence than ever before, I am "awake" to my old patterns and potential blocks more of the time, and I am constantly working on and adjusting my thoughts and behaviours to be more in line with my Authentic Self.

I am clear that I am valuable simply because I'm on this Earth, and not because I'm a successful something or because others like me. It's a very different way of being, and it feels comfortable and right for me.

It has been an incredible journey so far, and I am grateful for it all. I am also learning to be more comfortable in the "not knowing" about the future. I am, after all, manifesting it in each moment as I live authentically, more of the time.

I DISCOVERED THE FEELING OF INNER PEACE

HOW TANA INSPIRES INNER PEACE

Tana Heminsley is a thought leader, author, and integral coach with a focus on Authentic Leadership and Emotional Intelligence. In 2013 she published her first book "Awaken Your Authentic Leadership – Lead with Inner Clarity and Purpose".

Tana is the recipient of the International Coach Federation Vancouver Chapter 2016 Coach Impact Award. This is the highest award category in British Columbia for coaching excellence for individual partnership (Coach Impact) level. She is an executive and an entrepreneur with more than 30 years of experience building businesses and developing leaders.

During this time, Tana studied how individuals overcome childhood trauma to go on to become successful organizational leaders. She researched extensively the inner journey of leaders and how it relates to long-term behavioral change and recovering from unhealed issues on their path to Inner Peace.

You can discover more about Tana at leadauthentic.com

INTRODUCING
DIANA REYERS

Photo by ML. Kenneth

I had the pleasure of meeting my dear friend and mentor, Diana Reyers, in 2016. I have a small event's planning and consulting business, and she requested a meeting to discuss an up-coming event. I had no idea when I agreed to the meeting, she would become one of my closest friends. As she described Daring to Share, it became very apparent that she was very passionate about community and connection. In terms of the nuts and bolts of the event, I expressed to her that it sounded like she had everything under control so, what did she need me for? "To share a story," she laughed. I immediately agreed to be a storyteller at that very first Daring to Share event here in Oceanside.

Diana is driven, practical, passionate, organized and also one of the most loving, caring, compassionate people I know. She will wear herself ragged as she always makes herself available to her tribe, as a friend, a mentor, a coach or sometimes, just a friendly ear. Her laugh and enthusiasm are as contagious as her easy smile. As a fellow Meyers-Briggs' ENFP, we have this incredible synergy. No goal too lofty, we shoot for the stars!

This book came to fruition because of her drive and her passion and I am very honoured to be a part of it and feel very blessed to be part of Diana's world. Knowing her has changed the trajectory of my life in so many ways and I remain forever grateful .

You are about to experience Diana's Story[6] of
From There to Here **and how she discovered the feeling of**
Truth   *Scott De Freitas-Graff*

---

[6]This Chapter is an excerpt from the soon to be published *Daring to Share; My Road Trip to Truth* by Diana Reyers

From There to Here;

TRUTH

By Diana Reyers

Truth ™

Diana's Story

Throughout my life, my perception of truth has been my greatest struggle. It created chaos in my mind, in my life and within my closest relationships. The ambiguity of not knowing if my thoughts are real or fake, right or wrong, accepted or rejected took me to the closest feeling of what, I believe, insanity must feel like.

There were many times I sat in a state of questioning everything I thought, and other times when I believed thoughts that were complete fantasy. These latter beliefs were the ones that caused me the most grief and almost destroyed one of the most meaningful relationships I ever had with my mother. Over time, our perception of each other's intentions became slanted, and without, initially, having a conversation around the confusion created, we sadly spiraled into a dysfunctional relationship.

Eventually, we repaired the damage we created, but living through this process was painful for both of us; it became the greatest From There to Here within my Authentic Road Trip as I moved diligently towards my ultimate Truth. I vowed that I would fight to never create this turmoil within either of my children's lives. And yet, I believe I almost did.

I was meant to move through the joy of creating a deep connection with my mother, the brief, yet tumultuous breakdown of that bond, and then the eventual repair of it. I believe the intention of the universe was for me to learn great lessons by experiencing the painful parts, as well as, the joyous ones. The wisdom I discovered through this 50 plus year process has supported me within the deep connections I established with my own 2 children. Having the shoe on the other foot motivated me to reflect deeply about how I wanted to show up within my children's lives as they moved from a child's need for dependence to an adult's yearning for independence. I saw how the way I interpret and respond to my children's transition into adulthood greatly affects both of them, as well as me. Each of our perceptions of the truth can either support or hinder us. I know this because the way in which any of the relationships in my life unfolded was a direct reflection on how I responded to them and the other person involved responded to me.

I began my path in the world as a child who craved approval. When I received approval, a surge of energy moved through my body like a lightning bolt; I felt loved, and this became my truth. As a result, approval became my motivation to experience love, and people pleasing became my developed pattern while seeking approval. As a child, my mother became my love lifeline because she provided me with the positive feedback I yearned for. She made me feel that I was exactly who I should be, and I never felt like I needed to be anything other than how I showed up when I was with her.

Back then, my father was a shift worker at a local factory, and when he worked the midnight shift, I tiptoed into my parents' room at sunrise before he got home and slipped into bed with my mother. Keeping her eyes closed, she reached over to me and we held hands while I lay beside her. I felt connected to her and safe within her reach, and I believe she felt the same. Right now, I feel the warmth of her hand and the love she provided through her touch and this tiny gesture of physical connection.

By the time I reached the age of 4, I idolized my mother, and her presence and approval became a necessity for my creative self to be nurtured. My imagination motivated most of how I showed up in my safe little world, and my mother encouraged me to openly express all the stories and characters that popped into my head. I played endlessly in my bedroom with my dolls and stuffed animals. One might think I was playing 'house' but, I was engaging in conversation with them, telling them tales I conjured up in my mind with them replying the way I wanted them to.

We had a whippoorwill tree in the backyard, and I loved to lay underneath it while staring at the clouds. I discovered so many stories floating above me and equated the sky to a huge storybook provided by God. I often wondered how he picked the stories he offered as they changed from one day to the next. One day, I heard my parents talk about the whippoorwill tree, and how the roots could be a problem as they might grow under the foundation of the house. I expressed my deep concern to my mother about losing this place that ignited my imagination.

The tree was never cut down and it remained my sanctuary. I'm not sure if my mother ever talked to my father about my worry about the tree, but at that time, I felt my mother was a warrior and she had protected this beautiful tree and my time and space with the clouds.

My mother protected and fostered my sensitive, creative side as she encouraged imaginative play, art and conversation with me. For a whole year, while my two older sisters went off to school I had her all to myself. We did chores together, and she made it fun by playing music and chatting with me as we dusted or did the dishes together. Her love of music inspired mine, and I later performed for my family by singing along with my parent's favorite singers, Dean Martin, Petulia Clark, Bobby Darin and Frank Sinatra. On Sundays, after church, my mother piled 4 records on the hi-fi and I stood on the ottoman while holding the pestle part of a mortar and pestle set my father brought home from Indonesia; the pestle was my microphone. My sisters joined me, but I always wanted to be the lead singer, front and center. My mother sang along, and I bathed in her beautiful smile as she watched intently and enjoyed my performance.

At this point in my life, my mother provided me with everything I needed, love, acceptance and connection which all developed into self-confidence. We had a great gig going on there at home, and I was comfortable with it being just me and her.

"I felt safe at home and never imagined that I would ever feel the loneliness of introversion that comes with the perception of being different from others."

But, life evolves as it does, and I don't know why I thought

I would not have to go to school like my sisters did. I was living in a bit of a la-la land mentality ignoring my inevitable entry into society. Denial would later provide me with a way to get through some of my worst fears. So, when my mother announced that I would be going to Kindergarten and how fun it would be, my heart sank. She told me there would be lots of children and toys to play with, that my teacher was nice, and I would learn a lot. I told her I didn't want to go to school, I didn't care about playing with other kids, I had my own toys at home, and I didn't need to learn anything. Like most children, I didn't win that argument.

The first day of school arrived, and we walked to the Kindergarten just blocks from our house. I'm sure my mother felt my nervousness, and in an attempt to distract me, made conversation about the pretty flowers and how blue the sky was. None of this was intriguing to me because I was distracted by the unknown. I just wanted to continue living in my imaginary existence being at home with my mother. I made one final attempt at getting out of this predicament with a stern, "I don't want to go to Kindergarten," my mother replied with an equally adamite, "You're going to have a good time!!" It wasn't a question, and I could feel there was no room for argument. The decision was made, and we headed silently down the street to meet my teacher, Mrs. Roach. This is my first recollection of feeling the need to be right within my relationship with my mother.

I know that, subconsciously, I was worried about not having my mother with me. More specifically, I feared not having my her there providing me with the approval I was accustomed to and that provided me with the security I felt I needed. At this young age, I couldn't cognitively determine or articulate what I was feeling, but the anxiety I experienced was the result of my emotional discomfort of leaving my mother's side. The perception of my anxiety was that I needed my mother with me, along with her constant approval in order to survive emotionally and be loved.

I spent the next 8 months going to Kindergarten, and I made a few friends, but I always had a feeling that I was much different from them; not only did I look different, but I really believed that I thought and felt differently as well. Mrs. Roach took on the role of my nurturer and friend during the hours I was with her. She was like my mom because she encouraged my creative side and I, in turn, accepted this as approval. I was happy and with gratitude, yet sadly, 1965 would remain the best school year of my entire life. My mother did the right thing transitioning me into the real world, and I was blessed to have Mrs. Roach as my teacher and friend. But, as the end of that summer approached, my mother told me I was going to the big school in September. Of course, I knew that was coming but, I was good at ignoring things that made me nervous. Change was one of them.

My mother told me about all the wonderful things I would experience and all the old friends I would see there and the new friends I would make. So, off I went to the first day of school feeling optimistic and excited. My mother was right, there were old and new friends but, my initial experience was not so positive. As soon as I stepped on the playground, my stomach did a flip as I felt an icky feeling of being different. Just like on my first day of Kindergarten, I was confused and found myself trying to make sense of my wanting to run away from what I saw and how it made me feel. What I saw were many cute girls scattered around the yard. Some were skipping, some on the playground equipment and some standing on the pavement close to the building. All of them seemed to be engaging in an activity, and all seemed to belong to the group they were surrounded by. Again, that feeling of chaos and not understanding but, I didn't say anything, I just stood there absorbing and fighting the discomfort. I now know the anxiety I experienced came from, yet, another perception my mind interpreted about what I saw before me; I was an outsider. This became a feeling of disapproval and being unloved.

What I now know for sure, is that a perception only became real for me when I believed it. As a little girl with squinty eyes, a long nose, a pixie haircut and scrawny body, I believed that how I looked determined the measurement of my value to my peers, and I was different than every girl within my view. In my mind, I saw groups of friends all together with no one asking me to join them. I saw 'girl next door' beautiful girls with big brown eyes, little curled up noses and long hair tied up in pony tails. Every ounce of my being told me that this was not a good thing, and this began a long journey living with the belief that I was not good enough without the approval of others.

I don't think my mother ever knew how I felt because I never told her. I didn't want to show her that I was weak, sad or insecure; I wanted to show her that I was strong and felt great joy in life like she did. My need for her approval overrode the fact that I knew she was a good mother, a nurturing mother, and one who would sit and discuss things with me if I needed her to. I never gave her the opportunity to do that because my need for the security she provided me created my belief that she did not want to hear about my fears and that I would lose her approval if I shared them, I would lose her love.

At some point, after enduring the wrath of the nuns and the Catholic elementary school system in the 60's, I survived my insecurities and lack of self-worth around my classmates and graduated transitioning into high school. One day after school as I stood amidst the crowd of students waiting for the school bus, I experienced a feeling of desperation as I realized how alone I was. It was at this time and in that moment that my feeling of loneliness brought the warrior out in me. Subconsciously, my introverted-self decided it was time to learn how to adapt and find the human connection I craved within an extroverted world. I became stoic like my mother and came to the conclusion that I needed to embrace my distinctive characteristics and nurture them. I found solace in those differences; the very thing that I thought caused my lack of self-confidence provided me with strength. I was so starved for the loving energy that comes from deep friendships that I transferred my need for approval by figuring out a way for my peers to embrace my unique way of being, I discovered a survival method to fit in and not be that person who had no friends and sat alone in the cafeteria.

I became super creative in my efforts to fit in, and by the time I reached high school, I embraced my love for Barbra Streisand and the fact that this woman didn't resemble any famous person at that time but, was considered beautiful, talented and a superstar; she was adored. She showed up within her uniqueness and didn't seem to feel the need to change anything about herself. My feelings of inadequacy were consoled by envisioning myself as her; I already owned her likeness by way of similar facial features, and I permed my hair to further emulate her 1976 Star is Born persona.

Although, this provided me with the ability to function socially, I found myself immersed in a dysfunctional pattern of achieving self-confidence by emulating others. As a chameleon, I felt the approval of others but, realized this was an attempt to fit in by using how I looked to gain approval, a new perception that my physical-self provided the value of worthiness. I wanted to commit to being different but, in a genuine way that embraced my uniqueness without trying to be like someone else. I just didn't know how to do that.

At the time, pretending to be someone else and living in an imaginative world, provided me with the safety of superficial self-confidence. But, later, as I entered young adulthood, it became a chaotic whisper in my over-thinking mind that I was not good enough unless I was like someone else. My perception of reality and truth became distorted, and more confusion set in. I abandoned the idea of university, experienced several failed relationships with guys who cheated on me, and who I allowed to take advantage of my people pleasing nature while seeking their approval. I was sad, lonely and incredibly disillusioned about who I was and where I was headed.

"I came to the conclusion that there was nothing about me that anyone, including myself, would approve of because none of me was real. I realized that I allowed my need for approval to affect every decision I made.
I had no idea what I believed to be my truth."

And then, at the age of 22, I met my life partner, Hank. We fell in love over long car rides and conversations; I felt at home with him. He is a listener, I am a talker. As a runner and triathlete, he became my role model and guide towards healthier living and we enjoyed an active life style, the company of friends and time spent with one another. Although I was happy within my relationship, I struggled terribly with understanding who I am without someone else's approval. For a while, I felt the need to transfer my need for my mother's approval to a need for my husband's. Like a drug, I was addicted to the approval of someone else in order to feel loved, and so, I shifted this perception to the person I felt loved me the most at the time, my husband.

I began to feel the need to be released from the dependence I created on my mother's acceptance of me and wanting to make her happy at all costs. I found I was doing things for her, agreeing with her, and saying things to her to meet her expectations but, didn't reflect how I would otherwise show up from my heart and soul. Strange and uncomfortable sensations arose within me when I showed up in my pleasing mode. I began yearning to understand myself and what inspired me; I wanted to get to know myself from my inside out. Hank understood my new want for autonomy, and he encouraged my independence. I began my journey of self-discovery and expressing myself through art and writing. He, quietly and patiently, encouraged me to find my best self, to do things that made me happy, and he cheered on the expression of my creative side. I pursued many career paths and he always supported my choices and job changes which were many as I tried to discover my Authentic path. We got married when I was 24.

The shift into what happened next remains a mystery to me as I believe my mother and I began a dance that we could have avoided had we both understood what was happening at the time. I began, more often than not, to prove my mother wrong when she tried to have a conversation with me. When she expressed how she liked the same things I did or resembled me in any way, I somehow felt the need to dispute it all. Looking like her, being like her, enjoying her company, all the things that made me feel loved and approved of before, were the exact things I was repelling. My greatest regret about this is that I didn't sit down with her and have a conversation about how I felt or what my intentions were. I hadn't reached a level of awareness that provided me with the clarity about how to talk about this; I felt she wouldn't approve.

Pieces of what I wanted felt right while others felt uncomfortable and that feeling of confusion returned; I felt dis-compassionate and selfish, but I couldn't stop myself. This, rightfully so, triggered a need in my mother to defend herself. Her warrior mom came out from her fear of losing me, and it seemed to present by her seeking my approval. The tables seemed to have turned as the less approval I wanted from her, the more approval she sought from me. Was she now equating approval with love as well? We both began engaging in a pattern of competition and needing to be right, me by pulling away from her, and she by hanging on to me. It became emotionally draining for both of us. I love my mother very much, and the chaos created by the different perceptions we believed was destroying the beautiful connection we committed to and nurtured in the past.

At this time in my life, I know that throughout the personal evolution I was on I felt the need to create distance from my mother. It seemed to be a subconscious way for me to prove that I could feel and be loved without needing her approval. Being in the vortex of all the emotion, I didn't really understand what was happening so, I couldn't communicate to her why or how I was feeling – I just felt it. What I realize is that at that time, my way to survive this transition was to not need or even want her approval. I was growing into my autonomy, and with it came a yearning to emotionally detach from my mother. Hank seemed to hold that space by supporting me to be independent by discovering my own beliefs and committing to them. It didn't mean that my mother's beliefs were wrong, it's just that I felt I owned other values that deserved to be honored.

Today, I understand, and have deep compassion for my

mother because I know and understand the shift I created when I pulled away from her without any explanation. The bond we created together for 24 years suddenly changed, and I believe this created fear for her, the fear of losing me and all that we shared. Unfortunately, my mother's response to my pulling away, motivated her to hang on to me and my old ways of being and believing. I think it was difficult for her to let me go. At the time, my perception of this was that she was trying to control me and that she expected me to be the same as I had always been. My assumption of all this was that she didn't approve of who I was, and this translated into to a lack of love.

I struggled with this for many years and throughout the parenting of my own children. I created such a distorted story in my head of my mother's love for me that I vowed I would never attach the measurement of approval to the love from or for my children. I made a commitment that I would never expect them to be or do anything that didn't feel right for them, and I would support them to discover and commit to their own unique selves no matter the trade-offs along the way.

Many conflicts and disagreements with my mother arose over the years, and I finally found that I did not have the capacity to continue living the way we were. I came to a point in time when I had to let go of all the fear, anger, and resentment that we built up between us. After a particularly heated argument on the phone, my husband told me what so many others in my life said to me before, "You just have to let this go!" I left the house and got in my car. I decided to go to a place that provided me with the stillness I needed to recalibrate. As I drove to the yoga studio, I began chanting out loud, "Let it go." I repeated this out loud for 20 minutes and once I arrived on my mat, I found myself repeating the words in my head over and over again, "Let it go. Let it go." It became a meditation of sorts, and I felt a surge of calm come over me. As I began my practice, I couldn't stop repeating the words as they seemed to provide me with the comfort I needed. 10 minutes into the hour-long practice, I moved into a state of subconsciousness, and I don't remember anything after that. My next conscious recollection was finding myself sitting in the lobby of the yoga studio in the middle of a conversation with a group of fellow yogis and the instructor.

I was baffled about how I got to this bench engaging in a conversation I didn't remember starting. I didn't remember anything past the first downward dog of the class. I asked the instructor what happened, and, not understanding why I was asking, she explained that I moved through my practice like never before, including going deep into the pigeon pose. This intrigued me because the pigeon pose focuses on the hips, and it is believed that one stores deep emotions, feelings of anxiety, and fear and sadness within relationships in the hips until they are brought to the surface to allow a release. The pigeon pose is a way to accomplish this and it has always caused me great physical discomfort due to the stiffness in my hip joints. It would seem that I was able to release that stiffness through finally letting go of my need to be right with my mother.

"I had a choice that day, either manifest my perception of needing to be right, or
let go of the perception of the fear of being wrong."

Reaching emotional capacity moved me to choosing to let go of my fear, and I experienced the freedom of being released from my prison of perception.

I felt euphoric. I could not believe the emotional freedom I felt after that class and the transformation I experienced. I knew that reaching the peak of my emotional capacity and my mantra of "Let it go" lead me to my destination of Here. I finally let go of all the shit I carried with me for so many years. I no longer felt the push-pull of being right or wrong. It was all a little confusing to me, but it also felt like the old yogi speak; it felt kind and necessary, and it felt like the truth to me.

At that time, with my mother in Ontario and me living far away in Kelowna, British Columbia, I was working with an amazing life coach, Chelsey Marie[7]. She supported me in continuing to see my mother in a different light, with a different perspective, and one inspired by compassion, but mostly from the truth. I eventually came to a place of forgiveness, forgiveness for my mother and forgiveness for myself, and from that day on, the way I responded to my mother, anything she said or did, was with love and kindness.

Chelsey Marie suggested I practice 30 days of gratitude for my mother. I agreed and every morning after I journaled, I wrote one expression of gratitude to my mother. Each of them came from a genuine place deep within my heart and, after the 30 days, Chelsey asked me how I felt about sending them to my mother. I said I would with the intention of healing the past for both me and my mother. I sent them by regular post and let go of any expectations of how she would react to them. Not to my surprise, she called and thanked me for the lovely letter she received.

"You see, my mother is a kind and loving person who, just like me, yearns for the approval of others. We are very much the same as we both share the perception that Approval equals Love."

---

[7]Find Chelsey Marie at chelseymariecoaching.com

We are both enthusiastic about life and see adventure with all the world has to offer. We equally love the feeling of connection that is presented when we embrace the gathering of family and friends around a dinner table with good food and drink. We enjoy the camaraderie of being the same while at the same time, celebrating each other's differences. We are incredibly alike, which is why we created such a strong bond with each other in the first place, and yet we are very different, which is why we grew apart for a little while. Although I gradually mistrusted my perception of approval being the foundation of feeling loved by my mother, it, ironically, ended up being my truth all along. I just needed to find clarity about what approval meant to me, then learn to trust how it felt, and finally discover that seeking approval is not such a terrible thing after all, especially when it provides the feeling of love and ultimate truth.

My daughter, Olivia, now 24 years old, was married to the love of her life on Father's Day, June 17, 2018. Since the announcement of her engagement just over a year ago, I moved through one of my most reflective transitions. Although, I didn't want to admit it, my greatest insight through this time is that I realized my daughter and I began leading the same path my mother and I moved through with Olivia pulling away and me responding by feeling like I had to hang on. As soon as I experienced this feeling of déjà vu, I took a deep breath and stepped back in order to digest what I was experiencing. I wanted to be careful not to repeat history by temporarily destroying this beautiful relationship I have with my daughter. I did not want to lose my daughter by feeding into my ego and my fear and creating false perception.

33 years later, I understand what my mother went through because I experienced the same thing with my daughter, the

feeling of losing someone you love so dearly. My daughter began to pull away and I began to hold on to her for dear life as she started her Road Trip from There to Here, out into the world of adulthood, making her own decisions and committing to her own values while creating new ones together with her husband. She is discovering a whole new side of herself, her true self while understanding and finding clarity about what is right and what is wrong for her. It is my time and my choice to step back and honour her as she transitions into her own way of being, to shine and to feel confident and safe about how she thinks and feels. My way is not necessarily her way, and how I perceive her pulling away determines how I choose to respond to it. I feel and know that hanging on to her will push her away, while letting her fly and simply being here to love her will support her in being who she is meant to become. I must trust her as her own perceptions are hers to experience, learn from and experience.

And so, I will not hang on to the way we used to be, but rather let her go while giving her the freedom of her right of passage. I will offer her the space she needs to grow emotionally and fly freely through her evolution. I do not want either of my children to feel the uncomfortableness of being different, but rather the comfortableness of being unique. I want them to know that they can make their own decisions and I trust that they will choose their truth and commit to live within it. I am proud of them and I approve of all they have become; they are my love and my light.

I DISCOVERED THE FEELING OF TRUTH

HOW DIANA INSPIRES TRUTH

Diana Reyers is a Connector and Human Advocate. All her life she craved and discovered the healing power of community and human connection. She believes experiencing discomfort is necessary for emotional survival and growth.

"One Uncomfortable Conversation Provides
Ten Years of Wisdom."
~ Diana Reyers

Diana considers herself an equal amongst humanity. She knows that committing to leading an authentic life requires great courage and can be lonely at times. Using truth as her guide, she is empowered to show up as her best self, void of self-deception and judgement. Her greatest victory is persevering past false perceptions in order to experience connection by escaping the chaos of expectation, a place so dark she often felt she would never be freed from its imprisonment.

As a storyteller and writer, Daringly Mindful Diana shares her stories of grabbing her courage to choose personal truth while disclosing all the trade-offs along the way. She celebrates her victories and, unapologetically includes her U-turns and imperfections with humour, humility and grace. Diana Reyers Connects Humanity Through The Art of Storytelling by bravely sharing her Truth with the world.

You can discover more about Diana at daringtoshare.com

PRAISE FOR
THE CONNECTOR

TM

*"Diana can be best summed up with one word – Authentic.
She is a true beacon for living a life built by design not by
default, and her ability to stir others through a simple
conversation is pure magic.*

*Life is made up of a series of twists and turns and along that
journey are patches of wilderness that must be navigated in
order to find one's authentic self.*
*Diana shows us that this fountain of authentic youth can
happen at any age, provided that the journey is committed,
and the heart is open.*

*Growth can happen alone or through simple conversations
with strangers; we all have a story to tell, and through that
sharing we grow. Nobody better exemplifies this than
Ms. Reyers and her ability to draw human souls together
as one by the simple act of sharing and conversation."*

Jim Gardiner, Performance Coach
Life | Wellness | Business – TV host and creator of
The Inspirational 30 and Can Ordinary Inspire

DIANA REYERS
THE CONNECTOR

Photo by ML. Kenneth

Diana Reyers is a retired Authenticity Coach, a Storyteller, an Author and, what she considers her most impactful role, a Human Advocate.

Diana discovered that the tools of conversation are key elements within human connection. She sought and found them through Tana Heminsley, CEO of Authentic Leadership Global™ in Vancouver, British Columbia, Canada. Over tea, during her first meeting with Tana, Diana had a deep knowing she was about to begin her Authentic Road Trip towards leading a truly authentic life.

Diana became a *Certified Authentic Leadership Program Facilitator™* and discovered her daily intention of supporting others by showing up in the world as her best self, consciously making decisions, big or small, in line with her values and beliefs while practicing emotional and social intelligence. She, consciously, became a Mindful Mentor with the understanding that showing up within her Truth is the key to connecting to herself, others and the universe.

Diana's continued life vision is to *Connect Humanity One Story At A Time* through her series of collaborative Daring to Share Books, along with, her partnership with Scott De Freitas-Graff as they offer the world The Event with Great Purpose; Daring to Share has evolved into The Movement.

Connect with Diana

Website/Blog: daringtoshare.com
Twitter: @dianareyers
Instagram: @daretosharepqb
Facebook: www.facebook.com/daringlymindful/
LinkedIn: www.linkedin.com/in/dianareyers